Conversations With My Unbelieving Friend

Conversations With My Unbelieving Friend

Michael C. Gayle

ELM HILL
A Division of
HarperCollins Christian Publishing

www.elmhillbooks.com

© 2020 Michael C. Gayle

Conversations With My Unbelieving Friend

All rights reserved. No portion of this book may be reproduced, stored in a retrieval system, or transmitted in any form or by any means—electronic, mechanical, photocopy, recording, scanning, or other—except for brief quotations in critical reviews or articles, without the prior written permission of the publisher.

Published in Nashville, Tennessee, by Elm Hill, an imprint of Thomas Nelson. Elm Hill and Thomas Nelson are registered trademarks of HarperCollins Christian Publishing, Inc.

Elm Hill titles may be purchased in bulk for educational, business, fund-raising, or sales promotional use. For information, please e-mail SpecialMarkets@ ThomasNelson.com.

Library of Congress Cataloging-in-Publication Data

Library of Congress Control Number: 2019920522

ISBN 978-1-400330140 (Paperback)
ISBN 978-1-400330157 (Hardbound)
ISBN 978-1-400330164 (eBook)

TABLE OF CONTENTS

Introduction	vii
Chapter 1	1
Chapter 2	9
Chapter 3	17
Chapter 4	35
Chapter 5	63
Chapter 6	69
Chapter 7	81
Chapter 8	89
Chapter 9	105
Chapter 10	125
Epilogue	139

Introduction

I have been operating in the corporate world for almost forty years at the time of writing. For most of those years, I have occupied executive positions and have interacted with executives from all over the world. This includes friends at similar and other levels in their own professions or careers.

I was raised in a typical Jamaican middle-class religious household. My parents were members of a traditional Church, as was I. I attended confirmation classes and was confirmed at age twelve. Truth be told, this church used real wine ("sherry" I believe) in their communion, and that was the main attraction to me at that time as confirmation allowed me to have a weekly sip of the "forbidden fruit," forbidden at least for a twelve-year old. As a young teenager, I attended church most Sundays and was part of a youth group which met on Friday evenings. Upon reflection, it is quite clear to me that the motive was more of social interaction than any real connection with Jesus. Nevertheless, the seeds of faith had been sown.

This faith actually first manifested itself in an unusual way, which some might argue was not a manifestation of faith, but stay with me here. At about the age of seventeen, I became disenchanted with what I saw around me in the church. I saw a number of adults who were very pious on Sunday mornings but who did not show any sign of piety whenever I encountered them during the rest of the week. In some instances, their behavior was not reflective of what would be expected of those professing

Christianity. I came to regard church as a social enterprise that was dishonest, disingenuous, and, even worse, blasphemous. Even though I did not really know God at the time, the seeds which had been planted in my heart lead me to rebel against being a part of this blasphemous pretense, and as such, I stopped attending church.

Fast-forward to adulthood. My wife had a similar religious upbringing but with a different denomination. She was not a Christian per se when we got married, but even more so than was the case with me, the seeds planted in her childhood lead her on a quest to find Jesus. She eventually accepted Him as her Savior, and with our two (eventually three) children in tow, she started attending church on a regular basis. She visited a number of churches before settling on a burgeoning independent evangelical church which would eventually become known as Christian Life Fellowship (CLF).

Through her membership in this church, I began to interact socially with several church members who had become an integral part of our circle of friends. In this group, I saw something which I did not see as a teenager in my family's church. I saw a group of people whose ethics and pattern of life were the same outside of church as it was in church on Sundays. Were they perfect? No. Were they flawed? Yes. Were they genuine? Absolutely.

This was a new experience for me. Over time, I had a series of discussions with several of my new friends, and little by little, my long-held, deep-seated skepticism about Christianity began to fade. For one, it became apparent to me that being a religious, churchgoing person was much different than being Christian. Going to church does not make someone a Christian, any more than going to a garage makes one a car. My wife and children went to church on most Sundays, and I stayed at home. She was somewhat embarrassed, I think, by the fact that many of the other families attended church, and to the casual observer, it was as if her poor children were fatherless. Nevertheless, I refused to go to church just for the sake of keeping up appearances. As was the case with my departure from my childhood family church, I again firmly held the view that I would be blaspheming and that God would be very displeased with me.

That unusual manifestation of faith again.

In 1994, in response to my wife's "encouragement" (read what you wish into that choice of words), I surrendered my life to the Lord and started a journey. To be clear, for me this was not like flicking a switch and suddenly having all of my skepticism disappear. Quite the contrary in fact. I found that interaction with my fellow believers exposed me to aspects of Christianity which I had not been previously exposed to and which further challenged my science-trained mind (I studied two years of physics and chemistry at a university and ended up in insurance, but that is another story).

My experience as a non-Christian was that in speaking to Christians, many of the arguments for Christianity which were put to me were not credible in my opinion. It seemed to me at the time that Christians were somewhat gullible and were merely repeating scripts which they could not support and which, in many instances, defied logic. Worse yet was their willingness to accept what seemed to be weak justification of these positions. None of this served to bring me any closer to God but had the opposite effect.

Now having embraced the faith, as a young believer, I commenced this journey and had the opportunity of speaking to many seasoned Christians and engaging in a lot of reading, research, and study, both formal and informal. I found that my position was gradually evolving. Whereas there were aspects of Christianity that I had flat out rejected in the past, I soon became prepared to accept the fact that there may be things taking place in a realm which I did not understand and could not comprehend through my science-biased lenses.

For example, there were a number of discussions with well-known and respected doctors who told me stories of miraculous healing in response to prayer. These were not conversations with strangers or fanatics (a word which I do not use here as a pejorative but rather to describe someone so committed to their own belief that they cannot rationally evaluate any other viewpoint or accept the possibility that they could be wrong if the evidence points in that direction). These doctors were friends and/or close associates whom I held in high esteem, both from a professional viewpoint and also from the perspective of personal integrity. If such people described having witnessed or even personally experienced miraculous healing, then I could no longer dismiss out of hand the possibility that something is happening beyond my ability to understand it. To do so would have put me firmly within the definition of "fanatic" which I outlined above (I will come back to these doctors' stories later).

So as time has passed and my quest has continued, I have found answers to many (but not all) of my areas of skepticism. As my faith grew, I came to terms with the fact that there are many questions which I will never understand in this life, and having accepted that, I am okay with it. This does not stop me from searching for answers, but rather, it allows me to move on whenever I have been unable to find a satisfying answer. This may seem like a "cop-out," another case of blind acceptance of something which cannot be proven. I would (and will in due course) argue that such an assertion is disingenuous at best. Many unbelievers who hold this view also accept the "fact" that the universe was created in a split second by a big bang, even though only a handful of people who have ever lived are capable of even beginning to understand the science behind that assertion.

Hmm! Never thought of that, did you?

In my interactions with friends and associates outside of Christendom, I often encounter skepticism such as I had experienced and negative reactions to what they perceive to be feeble attempts to convince them of the need for Jesus in their lives. I have become convinced that when we as believers approach witnessing or evangelism on such a basis, then we damage our Christian witness and do more harm than good.

With this book, I attempt to address some of these issues by setting out what I believe to be reasonable and credible responses to questions that unbelievers may have. The format is that of a series of conversations over a period of time between a fictitious friend and me. Even though the conversations have been fabricated, many of the issues covered arise out of discussions that I have had with a number of people over the years and was probably unable to adequately address at the time.

As mentioned earlier, I have come to terms with the fact that I will not find answers to all my questions, and similarly, I have not attempted to address some issues which the reader may have hoped that I would. Some of these issues are the subject of scholarly debate even within the realms of Christendom, and in the absence of something approaching consensus, rather than adding to the readers' confusion and uncertainty, I will just avoid them for now. For those that I do attempt to address, I would ask that the reader approach the issues with an open mind and hold them to the same level of scrutiny that they hold other everyday issues to rather than to an unreasonably higher standard. The discussions with my friend are based on the fact that he is highly skeptical but is open to a fair and reasonable debate rather than merely trying to win an argument.

My journey has been gradual, but there are still many areas where I am seeking answers, and it is my hope that this book will help the readers take a few positive steps on a journey of their own.

It is not my assertion that the answers which I give represent original thought on my part. Indeed, most if not all will represent the outcome of research or recollection of discussions which I have heard or literature which I have read in the past. Where I am able to identify the source, I will make the appropriate references and acknowledgment. It is likely that there may be statements which reflect material which I have encountered in the past and which I firmly believe to be accurate but cannot necessarily provide a reference to the source. It is not my intention to try to plagiarize someone else's work, and hence, I will do my best to maintain the integrity of the book.

At the end of the day, the most important thing is to get the Word of God into the hearts of as many people as possible. To God be the Glory.

I do not lay claim to any impressive theological pedigree. In fact, my theological pedigree is somewhat limited, bordering on nonexistent. At the time of writing, I am in the process of pursuing a Masters in Theological Studies through the Southwestern Baptist Theological Seminary, Ft. Worth, Texas, even though I am not a Baptist. This is being conducted in collaboration with the newly formed Northwestern Caribbean Baptist Theological Seminary in the Cayman Islands where I currently reside.

I do not have any specific objective in mind, which is driving me to do these studies and will be past sixty years of age by the time I complete the course. I am merely one who loves the Lord and who is seeking to be able to defend His name wherever and whenever called upon to do so. 1 Peter 3:15 exhorts us to "Always be prepared to give an answer to everyone who asks you to give the reason for the hope that you have."[1] I have the heart of an apologist and wish to equip myself to answer those questions and also to help others find answers to questions that they may have. I have heard the term "apologist" used in a derogatory manner to describe someone who makes excuses for someone or an unpopular belief. Whereas this may technically be a correct use of the term (marginally so in my opinion), in my case, I refer to the definition in the Merriam-Webster Dictionary as "one who speaks or writes in defense of someone or something." In my case, I am equipping myself to be a defender of the Christian faith.

I have been somewhat influenced by the work of renowned apologists, Ravi Zacharias and Dr. Norman Geisler, both of whom I have had the honor of speaking with. These occasions were more memorable for me than for them, and as such, whereas I remember them fondly, I would be very surprised if either of them does. Some of the underlying ideas which I put forward in my discussions with my "friend" have, in some way, been influenced by the works of the apologists mentioned above and others. In this regard, I have leaned on the book *I Don't Have Enough Faith to Be an Atheist* by Dr. Geisler and Frank Turek. I have also been influenced by the work of Lee Strobel who has written a series of books under the common theme, *The Case for...*, such as, *The Case for Christ*,

---

[1] All Scriptures quoted are from the New International Version (NIV) unless otherwise stated.

The Case for Faith, *The Case for a Creator*, *The Case for Easter*, and *The Case for Miracles*.

The difficulty that I have is that many of my thoughts have resulted from years of deliberation and I may propose arguments which had their genesis in someone else's work which I read or heard years ago, but in respect of which, I cannot recall the source. I say again, it is not my intention to improperly use anyone's intellectual property, and if there are any instances where I do not give the appropriate recognition, I humbly apologize.

Against this background, it is my hope that this book will help to answer some of the questions that people like me have had over the years. The intention is not necessarily to lead readers to Christ.

Please do not misunderstand me. That, of course, is the ultimate goal, and I would rejoice if even one person makes a decision for Christ as a result of reading this book. Having said that, my primary objective is to provoke the thoughts of readers by addressing questions that might hinder them from making a decision for Christ, if not now, then at some point in the future. In 1 Corinthians 3:6, the apostle Paul writes: "I planted the seed, Apollos watered it, but God has been making it grow." If I may be so bold as to put myself vaguely in the company of the apostle Paul, my intention is to plant the seed.

It has been my experience that too often, rational discussion and debate are overshadowed by preexisting biases. It is impossible to convince someone that a wall is white if, for instance, they are looking at it through blue lenses and either fail to or refuse to recognize and acknowledge that the wall appears to be blue, not because of the actual color of the wall, but rather because of the lenses through which they are looking at it. This is, of course, an oversimplification but is one which I hope serves to illustrate the point that I am trying to make.

Discussions on religion are almost always like that. People come into a religious discussion with a preconceived viewpoint, and the vast majority tend to stick to that viewpoint, regardless of the facts presented. This initial bias prevents them from being able to acknowledge facts presented, which may suggest that their perspective is wrong. Such a mindset usually manifests itself in debates where each party listens to an opposing viewpoint trying to find ways to attack it rather than trying to evaluate whether or not there is any validity to it.

So, when I say that it is not my intention to necessarily lead people to Christ, what I mean is that rather than trying to convince the reader that the "wall is white," what I am trying to do is to persuade the reader to recognize that he or she is wearing blue lenses. If they acknowledge this, then the next step is to encourage (not convince) them to take off the lenses and to arrive at their own conclusion as to the color of the wall based on all of the information which they are able to access without the filtering effect of the lenses.

In this regard, I like to think of this book as a "gateway" book. By this, I mean that it is not necessarily the book which will bring about a change in anyone's viewpoint, but hopefully, it can take readers to the point (the "gateway") at which they can reassess their current position, one way or the other.

The "conversation" is presented as being one between me and a fictitious friend by the name of Jack. I have chosen this name because, at the time of writing, I cannot recall any past or present close or casual association with anyone named Jack with whom I would have had any such conversations. As such, I hope to eliminate or at least minimize the possibility of inadvertently attributing any dialogue, viewpoint, statement, or opinion to any real person. If, by some chance, I have overlooked a real Jack in my life (a distinct possibility as a result of advancing years), sorry about that, Jack!

Though the meetings and conversations with Jack are fictional (as is Jack), my background information is more or less in keeping with the reality of my past. There may be instances where I have altered my personal facts for dramatic effect, but these will not affect the underlying story or objective. Such deviations, if they do occur, will typically be very minor or patently obvious, especially to those who know me. Again, there is no intention to deceive, just to facilitate the flow of the narrative. Having said that, there will be references to incidents which really happened and/or to conversations with real (as opposed to fictional) friends. In these cases, no names have been used so as to protect the innocent (or the guilty…?). No doubt these friends will remember some of these conversations.

I have included some references to specific scriptures which in my view are relevant to a given part of the conversation. For the most part, these have been done as footnotes and are taken from the New International Version (NIV) of the Bible, unless otherwise stated.

Even though the format of the book emphasizes conversations and the attendant prologues and epilogues, there are a few cases where I have found it useful to deviate from the script to include narrative or references at a detailed level which would not typically arise in a conversation. For instance, I may refer to articles or research and include information which one would not normally be expected to commit to memory. It is not that someone could not commit such things to memory, but an aging brain such as mine would probably not be able to. Such information is included in order to present the reader with what I believe to be useful information on the topic being discussed. I will usually make a note of such insertions, but there may be cases where I simply weave some of this information into the conversation.

Chapter 1

Jack and I have been friends for quite a few years. We are both well established in our respective careers. We are good friends but would not describe each other as close friends. We do interact socially on occasion, as do our families. Over these years of association, we have developed mutual respect for each other and respectful tolerance of each other's views on a wide range of topics including but not limited to politics, sports, food, and of course religious beliefs.

I am a born-again Christian and Jack, shall we say, is not. He describes himself as an atheist. I will debate this point with him later, but let us start with that. I am a Christian, and Jack is an atheist.

Ironically, we both have similar backgrounds. We were raised in homes that were regarded as religious. In Jack's case, it was under another traditional denomination. We both went through the process of going to church with our parents, most Sundays. We both attended preparatory and high schools run by churches. Between Sunday school at church and religious education classes at our respective schools, we both received grounding in the Scriptures.

Then, hormones kicked in.

In my case, my involvement in church activities continued until about age seventeen. I attended church most Sundays and was also a part of a youth group which met at the church on Friday evenings. An honest reflection reveals that social interaction rather than religious conviction was the driving force behind my involvement for the last few years of that period, but there came a point where the realities of teenage life overtook any advantages of church-based social interaction.

It is a scientific fact (at least, that's my story, and I am sticking to it) that teenage boys require a lot of sleep. Having to go to school during the week meant that weekend mornings represented the available windows in which I could secure this badly needed commodity. With Saturdays reserved for sports and general gallivanting, this meant that getting out of bed on a Sunday morning to get to church by 9:00 am was no longer an option. This was made even more challenging by the fact that on some of those Sunday mornings, I arrived home as the sun was rising to the great displeasure of my mother who was preparing to go to church as I was sauntering in at this unmentionable hour of the morning. I must confess an inability to understand her displeasure at that time. I had, after all, arrived home safely and in one piece. As I became a father, my own teenagers inflicted variations of this scenario upon me, and now I understand. The Lord has a sense of humor.

But I digress.

This increase in hormonal and commensurate nocturnal activity coincided with a growing disenchantment that I was experiencing with church. I can trace it back to the age of eleven or twelve when I was attending confirmation classes. This is a series of classes which youngsters in the church had to go through before being allowed to take communion. This is a transition which is in some ways (I guess) similar to the Jewish *bar mitzvah*. The classes were conducted by the reverend gentleman who was the rector at the church and served to lay a strong foundation.

There was one class, however, when we were taught that our bodies were God's temples, and as such, we were to take good care of them. In that regard, smoking was a sin because we were damaging God's temple. This had an instant impact on me because, at the time, my father was a heavy smoker. What had an even more substantial impact on me, unfortunately, was seeing the reverend gentleman go out to his car after the class, light up a cigarette apparently oblivious to the fact that we were looking, and then drive off into the night. What kind of message does this send to a young Christian? Do as I say, but not as I do?

This lurked in my mind for years, and as I approached the hormonal stages, I observed more and more instances of such apparent conflicts between what is said and what is done in the church, and I eventually convinced myself that participating in what I regarded as a disingenuous activity was quite blasphemous. As such, in a backhanded way, I was able to justify in my own mind not attending church.

Jack's journey seems to have been similar to mine, except that he stopped going to church a year or two before I did. In my case, I maintained an underlying religious inclination. I had a relatively typical teenage life involving most of the usual hijinks that teenagers get involved in. As an aside, in spite of many opportunities to do so, I managed to stay away from the use of marijuana. Never tried it. This was not because I necessarily thought it was wrong (teenagers have a warped moral compass anyway), but because I was determined to prove to myself that I could withstand peer pressure. Mission accomplished!

As we moved into young adulthood, tertiary education and fledgling careers beckoned. I settled down very early and married the love of my life at age twenty-three. By the time I reached age thirty, we were a few months away from our third child, and I was on my way to a promising career in insurance.

Jack remained single for a few more years and did not find his soul mate until he was thirty, by which time he was also well established in his career. Whereas I had maintained the abovementioned underlying religious inclination, Jack had done a complete about-face. He was so wholly disenchanted by what he saw as the hypocrisy in the church and of those who professed to be Christians that he had come to some faulty conclusions about Christianity which are common among unbelievers. Rather than setting them out here, I will allow them to emerge in my discussions with him.

Even though we were married in my family church, my wife's foundation was a little different, having lived for some years with relatives who attended another church. Like me, she was not a practicing or active church attendee when we got married and, indeed, for some years after. Unlike me, she had a yearning to connect with the Lord in a personal way. Over a period of years, she visited a number of churches before settling on an independent Evangelical church near to our home.

She attended church on most Sundays accompanied by our three children, while I stayed at home, sometimes cooking the traditional Sunday meal but typically ensconced in front of the television, preparing for a full day of NFL games during the season. She begged me to accompany them to church. "People are wondering if the children are fatherless," she said. Or, "people thought that the man seated beside me was my husband," she said. Or, "can you come with us at least once in a while as a family activity?" she would ask.

I was not having it. I was absolutely firm in my resolve. With total sincerity, I held the view that going to church in order to maintain appearances would be more offensive to God[2] than not going at all, and as such, I refused to participate in such a charade. Was this just an excuse to avoid going to church? It could have been, but I genuinely don't think so. For me, church was what I turned my back on more than fifteen years before, and I had no intention of "wasting my time" in participating in an exercise of hypocrisy.

Having said this, I was always supportive of her quest (must have been that underlying inclination rearing its head again) and interacted socially with many individuals and families from her new church. Some of these families became and still remain some of our closest friends. Wise (or crafty) person that she is, my wife encouraged me to participate in periodic sessions with a group of men from the church, where the board game "Risk" was played for hours on end. This served to facilitate closer interaction with these men and to strengthen bonds of friendship. It also had the (no doubt intended) by-product of enabling me to see how these men operated outside of church and to observe or participate in

---

[2] (Galatians 6:7) "Do not be deceived: God cannot be mocked."

discussions with them. As a result, I was able to see what it looked like to "walk the Christian walk" rather than just to "talk the Christian talk."

I became comfortable in their presence, and without even realizing it, little by little, my anti-church sentiments, though still present, were being eroded. On a number of occasions, my new friends would engage me in quiet, nonthreatening discussions in which the question asked was some variation of, "So, Mike, you spend a lot of time among us. You are just about one of us. What is preventing you from committing your life to the Lord?" My answer was typically some variation of, "when the Lord is ready for me, He will send for me." I recall one such instance when a doctor friend of ours visited me at my office, and as she sat in front of me and engaged me in such a discussion, I actually felt light-headed. It was as if the presence of the Lord was manifesting itself in my office, and I must confess that I was a little alarmed by it.

Eventually, one night at home, my wife asked me (not for the first time) if I was ready to accept the Lord, and to her surprise, I said yes. We knelt beside the bed and she led me to the Lord right there. The following Sunday, she asked me if I would go to church with the family, and I agreed. My expectation was that I would just be one more unnoticed face in the crowd.

My expectation proved to be very wrong.

At a particular point in the service, the pastor (who by now was also a friend) announced to the church that I had accepted the Lord. There was loud and prolonged applause and shouts of joy, much to my embarrassment.[3] Unbeknownst to me, the church (or significant portions thereof) had been praying for my salvation, and as such, there was much celebration.

That represented the beginning of my walk of faith, a walk which I continue to grow in. Mine was not a radical, dramatic conversion as some have experienced. I experienced a gradual change in my lifestyle, and in due course, I embarked on a quest of my own as I sought answers to the

---

[3] (Luke 15:10) "In the same way, I tell you, there is rejoicing in the presence of the angels of God over one sinner who repents."

myriad of questions that I had and set out to know the Lord better and to draw closer to Him.

It was not a smooth walk. There were bumps in the road. Many bumps. In the course of my walk, I learned many things. I learned that being a Christian does not mean that life is going to be more comfortable. I learned that being a Christian does not mean that one is perfect. I learned that Christians are not perfect people who do not fall prey to the same human frailties as everyone else, nor are they expected to be. I learned that all have sinned and fall short of the Glory of God.[4] I learned that He expects us to strive to be like Him, but He does not expect us to achieve perfection. I learned that what He expects of me is faithfulness and not perfection. I learned that He accepts me and loves me even with my multitude of flaws. I learned that there is nothing that I can do to earn His love. He makes it available to me by His grace.

And I learned that many of the views and opinions on Christianity which I had held for years were not accurate.

Jack, in the meantime, did not find himself in the same sort of social environment that I did. Both he and his wife maintained active lives, and I regard them as good, kind, and caring people. I had also thought of myself as a good, kind, and caring person. Indeed, based on my own experience, I was able to appreciate that "good" people are among the hardest to convince that they need the Lord in their lives. Because they are "good," they do not believe that they have any need for a redeemer, and those who may believe in an afterlife hold the view that being "good" is enough to get them into heaven, without having to go through the "trouble" of getting involved in church activities.

That was indeed true in my own case where I thought that I had all bases covered by being "good." I once even had a good laugh (forgive me Lord) at the fact that a member of my staff once thought that I was a Christian (before I actually became one) which, in my mind, was a reflection of my "goodness."

---

[4] Romans 3:23

It is sometimes easier to reach someone who is not "good," who knows that he or she is not "good," and who is struggling as a consequence of being not "good." Such a person is in desperate need of help and will be more receptive to an offer of salvation as they recognize their own wretchedness.

Which brings us back to Jack.

Jack was a good person. Jack was not suffering. Jack had a good life. And Jack had bad memories of church and church people stretching back to his teenage years.

Since becoming a Christian, I have had several superficial discussions with Jack. In most instances, he teased me about my Christianity, in a good-natured way but, nonetheless, in a way which reflected his underlying anti-Christian leanings. It was never malicious or vitriolic, but I was always reluctant to pursue the discussions because I did not think that I had enough substantial information to enable me to engage him in a discussion of substance. Yes, I knew all of the typical arguments that we hear and are taught, but in reality, I found that some of them were not necessarily strong and convincing arguments and held the view that attempting to defend my beliefs with weak arguments did more harm than good to my witness.

I set about cataloging my own misconceptions and researching responses which I would have found compelling. Armed with this information, I was now ready to engage Jack.

Chapter 2

Jack and I would have lunch together every couple of months or so. On one of these occasions, I decided to look for an opportunity to start the discussion in as nonthreatening a way as possible. It presented itself soon enough when we were discussing an item carried in the media (details of which are not material to this discussion), and Jack commented:

"See, that is the problem with you Christians. You will believe anything, whether it can be proven or not. As an atheist, I would never have believed a fishy story like that."

I recognized that he had opened the door for me and immediately recalled an approach described by Dr. Norman Geisler and Frank Turek in their book *I Don't Have Enough Faith to be an Atheist*.

"So you're an atheist, are you?" I replied. "Would you be open to a little discussion on that point?"

"What point?" he responded. "The news item?"

"No," said I with a twinkle in my eye (not really relevant but I thought that the turn of phrase was catchy). "Not the news item, but about you being an atheist."

He immediately became suspicious and went on the defensive. "Oh no," he said emphatically. "You are just trying to draw me into another of your attempts to convert me, and I really have no interest in that."

I knew that the discussion was delicately poised at this stage, and my next few statements would make or break the attempt to engender dialogue. I also knew that he was an intelligent person and decided to appeal to his intellectual curiosity.

"I am not trying to convert you Jack," which was true. At that point. I was trying to break down barriers. If there was to be a conversion attempt, that would come somewhere down the line. "I am just hoping to have a discussion so that we can be sure that we are talking about the same thing when we converse and that you are not speaking about 'apples' while I am speaking about 'oranges.' The apples and oranges situation does not lend itself to a constructive discussion."

"Fair enough," he said. I could tell that he was still suspicious of my motives, but on an intellectual level, the focus had been shifted to that of a debate which he was sure that he could not lose. We had, after all, been having spirited debates on a wide range of topics for many years, debates which we both enjoyed. He settled back into his seat, ready for the challenge which he saw coming.

I started the discussion with, "You say that you are an atheist. An atheist is someone who does not believe there is a God, one who *knows* that there is no God. Would you say that this describes your position?"

"It describes it perfectly Mike. Like you, I grew up in the church believing in God, but as I got older and learned to think for myself, I came to the conclusion that there could not possibly be a God, not with all of the suffering and evil in the world. Christians believe 'fairy tales' written in the Bible, stories about things which are unverifiable and which they are expected to blindly believe, in *faith*. A lot of what they are expected to believe as miracles can be explained by *science* which is verifiable rather than just subject to blind faith. *If I cannot see it, hear it, taste, touch it, or smell it, I don't believe in it.*"

This was like a gold mine for me. Without even knowing it, Jack had opened up so many avenues for my discussion with him that I smiled. He must have thought that the smile was an acknowledgment of the strength of his statement as he smiled in return. I was reminded of the first time that I took my kids to a Toys R Us store, and they became confused by the wide selection of choices available to them. Too many options is not always a good thing.

But I digress.

Faced with this treasure trove of evangelistic opportunity, I chose my approach very carefully and decided to stick to the first point now. The rest could come later.

"So based on your statement Jack, you have been able to verify that there is no God. You have either done or reviewed exhaustive research and analysis and can confirm without a doubt that there is no God."

His smile faded as he began to sense that he was being trapped by his own words, but he bravely attempted to rebound from what he must have perceived as a minor setback. "Mike, you are splitting hairs. You know that it is not possible to prove that God does not exist, any more than it is possible to prove that the tooth fairy or the Loch Ness Monster do not exist."

"I agree Jack. So what you mean to say is that you do not think that God exists. You have strong doubts, but you really don't know if there is a God and believe that it is impossible for you to know. That does not make you an 'atheist.' It makes you an 'agnostic.'"

Having now confirmed that he had trapped himself, he laughed heartily, an admission of defeat. "I never thought of it that way Mike, but you are right. I am not an atheist. I am an agnostic. In retrospect, using that definition of an atheist, I cannot see how any honest, clear-thinking person can claim to be an atheist. That does not change my view, however. I will just modify my statement. As an agnostic, I would never believe a fishy story like that," he said triumphantly, convinced that he had snatched the proverbial victory from the jaws of defeat.

I, of course, recognized that what seemed like a small adjustment of terminology to him, in fact, represented a significant shift which could open the door to further discussion, if I proceeded carefully. And proceed carefully, I did.

Actually, proceed carefully I did not. I proceeded at full speed ahead.

"So having agreed on the apples and oranges, can we take a look at your position in a little more detail?" I asked.

"I am still not letting you convert me," he responded.

"No problem. I just wanted to examine some of the other aspects of your statement. It may be that in the same way that I was able to provide a different perspective to your 'atheism,' I may be able to provide a different perspective to some of your other assertions, a perspective which you may accept in the same way that you accepted the atheist/agnostic perspective."

I continued, "There are two things that I would ask of you. The first is that you do not treat this as a religious discussion per se. Discussions on religion and politics tend to be so heavily clouded by personal preferences and biases that a rational discussion proves to be very difficult. I have a lot of respect for you Jack, and I trust that you also have a lot of respect for me. If you and I were having a serious discussion and you told me that you saw a UFO land on the football field and aliens came out and looked around, then, because it was you telling me this in a serious discussion, I would not dismiss it as nonsense as would be the case if I had seen it on the Internet, for example, or heard it from any of a couple of our other friends." He smiled as he knew precisely which friends I was referring to. "I would conclude one of two things. Either Jack saw a UFO, and therefore my existing beliefs about aliens visiting earth have to be revisited or alternatively, Jack saw something which he genuinely believed to be a UFO. I would never conclude that you fabricated or imagined it. As such, my request is that you look at the information that I am going to share with you and not just reject it as being religious propaganda. If it is true, the truth will stand on its own—if you allow it to."

"The second request is that you treat this discussion fairly, just like you would any other topic. We sometimes hold religious discussions to a higher standard of proof or reason than we apply to everyday life. I am not asking you to accept weak arguments, but please do not set the bar at a level which is unreasonable."

"Underlying these requests is the premise that you really are interested in having a discussion and not an argument where you take the position 'well this is what I believe so do not try to confuse me with the facts!'"

After contemplating my requests for a few seconds, he responded, "I take your point, and I agree to accede to your two requests. As it stands now, I am firm in my convictions but am prepared to give your arguments a fair hearing. This does not mean that I am going to change my mind, though."

"Unless the facts leave you with no choice," I said.

"Unless the facts leave me with no choice," he agreed with a smile, a smile which suggested that he did not expect this to be a problem, a smile which was saying to me: "bring it on, Mike!"

"Ok. We are off to a positive start. Let us take it in small steps. We both have to get back to work, so what I propose is that we establish some fundamental points here today, and if you are sufficiently interested, we can have another discussion. If at the end of that discussion, there are still areas that we have not addressed to your satisfaction, we can meet again until we reach a point where you are comfortable with the outcome, one way or the other."

This drew immediate protest from him. "Now wait just a minute! I agreed to have a short discussion with you today, and you are trying to turn it into multiple sessions?"

"You will note that I said we would only continue if you wanted to. If, at any point, you are not sufficiently interested, then we can call a halt to the proceedings."

"That sounds reasonable," he responded. I had the distinct impression that he said that simply to bring the discussion closer to an end, safe in the knowledge that he would have no interest in continuing the conversation after today. Time would tell.

I reverted to my modified version of the Geisler and Turek approach.

"So when we started, you declared that you were an atheist and that you knew that God did not exist. After some discussion, you conceded that a rational, clear-thinking person could not affirm the nonexistence of God since that is a negative which cannot be proven. On that basis, you conceded that perhaps you were an agnostic rather than an atheist. The difference being that an agnostic's position is that he does not and cannot know if God exists. Would that be a correct assessment of where we are now?"

Having been trapped by his own words before, he was very careful with his answer. "Yes," he said, "but remember, my position has not changed. I still do not believe that God exists, but I just cannot prove it."

"Fair enough. Having agreed that you cannot know for sure that God does not exist, then this leaves the possibility that He does exist. Would you agree with that assertion? I am not at this point asking you to agree that He exists, just that it is possible that He exists. In the same way, we do not know for sure whether Nessie (Loch Ness Monster) does or ever did exist, but to the extent that we cannot disprove her existence, we are obliged to concede that it is possible that she does exist or did at some point." Here I was juxtaposing a theological phenomenon with a real-world phenomenon and appealing to his undertaking to apply comparable and fair assessment criteria.

He thought about this for a little while and said, "Yes, I can agree to that assertion. Not that God exists, but simply that in as much as I cannot know for sure that He does not exist, then that leaves the possibility that He does, even though I still believe that he does not. I just can't prove it."

"Good. Now having agreed that it is possible that He does exist, are you willing to take a look at facts which will help you to decide whether your original position is accurate or not? Are you prepared to accept the existence of God if the evidence points strongly enough in that direction? Before you answer, let me break it down a bit further. At times, such deliberation is clouded by the fact that that there are many religions which claim to have their own gods, and as such, the deliberation is clouded by attempts to differentiate between them."

"At this point, I am not asking you to make that differentiation. In its simplest form, I am first asking you to consider the existence of a creator, an intelligent designer who put it all together. I am not yet asking you to accept that this creator is the God that I believe in. That would be like exposing a student to basic algebra and then expecting them to solve calculus equations. They must first become comfortable with the basic algebra and then and only then can they gradually move on to calculus."

"If (when?) we get to the point where you agree that the evidence points towards the existence of a creator, then if you wish to continue, I will help you to look at evidence that this creator is the God of Jews and Christians," I concluded.

He had been listening carefully and responded with an equal amount of caution. "So you are in effect saying that what you are asking me here is not to consider evidence pointing to God in the Bible but just evidence of intelligent design by an unknown and unnamed creator?"

"Correct," I responded. "If we can get over the initial question of whether or not there is a creator, and if you are still interested in pursuing it, I am confident that I can provide compelling evidence in support of the Christian and Jewish God. The long-standing debate as to whether creationists or evolutionists are correct is often obscured by the fact that evolutionists disbelieve the creation story in the Bible, and as such, their evaluation of the facts is clouded by this obstacle. What I am hoping to do is to remove that obstacle and to present you with facts that you can analyze rationally. As such, it is only if we get to the point where you agree that there is some substance to my argument, and if you wish to continue our discussions, then we can continue. If not, then we can bring the discussion to an end."

"Those are two big 'ifs,'" he said, "but I agree to hear you out on that basis. Remember though, if we cannot get past the first stage, I am not interested in the second."

"There would be no point in proceeding," I agreed. "That is likely to be a longer discussion than we have time for now, and there are a couple other foundational points I would like to touch on before we leave."

What has been achieved so far is that what started out as an avowed atheist has shifted ever so slightly to the point where he is prepared to consider the possibility of the existence of a creator and that this creator may be God. This may seem like a small shift but was actually quite a large one.

I continued.

"Earlier in our discussion and in other discussions that we have had in the past, you have asserted that Christians exercise blind faith and are like sheep, following blindly a belief system which has no verifiable basis. They will believe in anything, whether it can be proven or not. With your permission, I would also like to approach this from two points of view. As was the case with the approach to the question of the existence of a creator, I would like to separate it into two distinct but ultimately related discussions, and as was the case with the creator, if we cannot get past the first point of discussion, then there will be no need to proceed to the second."

"The first point I would like us to look at is this. The term "blind faith" is often ascribed to Christians in a derogatory manner, but the exercise of this faith is actually not dissimilar to "blind faith" which we exercise in our everyday lives in matters not related to religious beliefs. In fact, as I go on to look at the second point, I will seek to demonstrate that the faith that we exercise every day is, in many instances, founded on the basis of even fewer facts and verification than religious beliefs. In this regard, the second point will be that contrary to your assertion as noted above, much of the so-called blind faith of Christians is actually based on facts which can and have been verified if the standards of usual scholarly verification are applied, rather than a standard to which only religious inquiries are sometimes held."

Having deliberated somewhat before agreeing to the approach to the discussion on a creator, he quickly saw a parallel in this proposed discussion on "blind faith" and readily agreed.

I did not want to overload him at this point, and I was convinced that much progress had been made, so we agreed to part on that note. I asked him to give some thought to what we had discussed and loosely committed to being in touch, leaving the door open for him to call me if he was inclined to do so.

It did not hurt that I paid for lunch.

Chapter 3

Two weeks passed and I had not heard from Jack. I was tempted to call him but was conscious of the fact that if I pushed him too hard, I may turn him away and decided to await a suitable opportunity for the follow-up approach. Sure enough, I ran into him in the supermarket as we were both carrying out duties duly delegated and assigned by our wives. We exchanged pleasantries, and I was pleased and a little surprised when he indicated that he had given some thought to our discussion and was looking forward to an opportunity to continue. Based on our brief conversation, I sensed that he had been doing some research on his own and may actually have been looking forward to recovering what he may have perceived as "lost ground" from our previous discussion. Nevertheless, I was presented with a willing participant, and we arranged to meet in a few days at his home.

As agreed, I arrived at his home on a pleasant Saturday afternoon, having used the intervening days to sort out the information that I was going to share with him. A discussion about whether or not there is a creator could be tricky, and I was aware of the fact that if not tactfully done, I would lose him at this stage. This takes me squarely into the debate of evolution vs. creation, a topic which was a potential minefield.

I resolved to try to avoid a discussion which was too technical while recognizing that if he took the discussion in that direction, then I would have not just to follow, but to lead. I made a mental note of the topics which I would try to avoid and came up with methods of avoiding them without seeming to be dodging the issue.

Truth be told, there were several issues which I did not have answers to and was still searching for my own answers. In such cases, I thought it would be better for me to tell him that I did not have an answer rather than put forward a position which I did not myself have confidence in and therefore could not defend. Too often, before I became a Christian, attempts were made to convert me by people using weak arguments and quoting scriptures they probably did not understand and sometimes incorrectly interpreted and/or cited. This was one of the things that kept me away from Christianity and made me regard Christians with suspicion. These were well-intentioned but misguided efforts which ended up doing more harm than good. I did not want to make that mistake in my discussions with Jack.

As we nibbled on sandwiches prepared by his wife, he led off the discussion.

"So," he said, "you plan to try to convince me that there is a creator."

"Not really," I responded to his surprise. I let him chew on that for a few seconds before I continued. "You are a reasonable person, and you have honored your undertaking to examine the facts with an open mind so far. I am going to present some facts to you and let you draw your own conclusions. Just to be clear, there are some topics where you may not get the response from me that you expect. There are topics where I myself am still searching for answers and also topics where I do not believe that the typical response will help you to arrive at an opinion, so I may avoid those. Included among these two areas are topics where there is no consensus within the Christian world, and if I do not have a firm personal position on those topics, I will not try to convince you of their validity."

"Fair enough," he said. "Tell me about your creator."

"Ok," I said. "Basically we are looking at two broad possibilities for the origin of the existence of life. We will examine both of them and try to determine which one seems to be reasonable and which one seems to be far-fetched. On one hand is the theory that living organisms are the result of a series of random events, and on the other hand is the proposition that all that we see around us, all forms of life that exist, have ever existed, and will ever exist, are the product of deliberate, detailed, complicated, meticulous design. Remember now, we are not at this point talking about the existence and work of the Judeo-Christian God. We are talking about a superior life-form which existed before life on earth, which, by a deliberate process of intelligent design, created the earth and all that is on it. I phrase it that way so that for the time being, we can remove religious biases from the deliberation process."

I took a sip of a delicious fruit smoothie while I allowed that to sink in. I detected a hint of mango and pineapple. And banana.

"Let me remind you of the ground rules that we agreed. You will approach the discussion with an open mind and treat the information just as how you would treat any other information that you are analyzing and not as a religious discussion." He agreed and continued to munch on his grilled cheese sandwich as I gathered my thoughts.

"As a young boy," I started off, "my father had a lot of books on his bookshelves. One of these books was Charles Darwin's *On the Origin of the Species*. It meant nothing to me as a small boy, but as I progressed to high school, I was formally introduced to this book and Darwin's theory of evolution which was considered to be the foundation of evolutionary biology. I was fascinated to learn about this theory, presented almost as an acknowledged fact. To a young scientifically inclined mind, it all seemed quite reasonable. Why wouldn't it? We were being taught this in biology class along with human anatomy, the structure of a flower, osmosis and diffusion, and many other equally fascinating scientific 'facts' and we all accepted these by faith." I had deliberately inserted the word "faith" into the dialogue

Jack smiled. He remembered classes like those as well.

"This is not a scientific discussion Jack, and in spite of a background in science in high school and university, I do not profess to be an authority on matters of science. I am going to share with you certain scientific information as I understand it, but I invite you to do your own fact-checking.

I am not asking you to believe anything that I say, just because I have said it. I will ask you to accept that anything I say, I believe to be true but am prepared to be as open-minded as I am asking you to be and to modify my position if the facts lead me to the conclusion that my original position may be incorrect."

He nodded his agreement, and I continued.

"The essence of Darwin's theory is that species evolve over the course of generations through a process of natural selection. According to his theory, the stronger ones would survive and the weaker ones would cease to exist. The survival of the fittest. Hence in his view, man and monkey evolved from a common ancestor. He did not assert that man evolved from monkeys as is sometimes claimed by his detractors. He was confident that future fossil finds would validate his theory, establishing a link between caveman and modern man and further establishing the link between man and monkey. He arrived at this theory having observed variations in species on a trip to the Galapagos Islands which, along with other research, formed the basis for his theory which we accepted by faith."

"I suppose you are going to tell me that Darwin's theory is wrong, that there is no such thing as evolution," he said.

Putting the ball back into his court, I restated my earlier approach.

"What I am going to do is present you with current information and ask you to arrive at your own conclusions. We now have the advantage of DNA analysis which helps us to better understand some of the underlying issues. What this analysis tells us is that caveman and modern man have distinctly different DNA, sufficiently different that scientists have concluded that there is no link between the species. Modern man did not evolve from caveman. This position is further strengthened by the fact that more than 150 years later, there have been no fossil finds which support Darwin's theory. The expectation was that scientists would have unearthed evidence of this gradual shift from one species to another. Instead, what has been found is the sudden appearance of new species without any link to previously existing species. The fabled 'missing link' is still missing."

"But didn't you say that he had observed such variation on the Galapagos Islands?" he asked, not triumphantly but now genuinely curious.

"What he observed," I answered, "was minor variation *within* a given species. This is what we now refer to as microevolution. It is thought that based on his 'micro' observations, he arrived at his theory by extrapolation from his evidence rather than by having empirical evidence. He was confident that such evidence would eventually emerge, but instead, the evidence which has emerged has refuted rather than supported his theory, a theory which in effect asserts macroevolution."

"So, the short answer to your question is that science supports the occurrence of microevolution but as of now has not unearthed sufficient evidence to support macroevolution. Let us take this beyond Darwin. A cornerstone of evolutionary theory is the premise that life started when a single cell was randomly formed. One popular theory holds that a source of energy was introduced into the right mixture of atmospheric chemicals in just the right combination, and the result was the first simple cell. This single cell grew and split into other cells, and thus the first primitive life-forms emerged. These life-forms then continued to evolve by a Darwinian mechanism until life as we know it developed."

"Of course, this premise conveniently overlooks the question, 'What (or who?) was the source of this energy?'. But even leaving that aside, for now, let us assume for the purposes of this discussion that it did actually happen. Let us assume that the right combination of oxygen, nitrogen, hydrogen, and carbon just happened to be activated by this energy source and created the first simple cell, a simple organism with a nucleus surrounded by some sort of cytoplasm, all kept in place by a cell membrane. This sounds feasible on the face of it, and we all accepted this by faith. It should not have been too difficult for a simple cell to be created if all of the necessary conditions were present and the 'stars were all aligned.'"

"Except for one little fact. The simple cell is not so simple after all. We are now told by scientists that even the simple cell is a very complex mechanism with DNA involving billions of bits of information which have to be arranged in a particular order for the cell to function. An article "The Awesome Worlds Within a Cell" written by Rick Gore in a 1976 publication by the *National Geographic Society* asserts: '[The instructions within the DNA of a single cell], if written, would fill a thousand 600 page books. This is just a single strand of DNA within the millions of such strands within a simple cell.'"

"The odds of such a complex mechanism being created by spontaneous generation are such that in the ordinary course of events, we would consider it to be impossible. For example, if we painted a circular target, say six inches in diameter, in the middle of a field and a pilot flying thirty thousand feet overhead asserted that he could drop a golf ball from that height into the center of the target in one attempt without the use of special laser or other guidance devices, most of us would conclude that the probability of him succeeding was so low as to render it a statistical impossibility. Technically, it could happen, but the chances of it actually happening are so minute as to render it able to be considered to be impossible, and no rational person would give any credence to the pilot's claim."

"Many scientists have attempted to estimate the odds of successful formation of a live cell by a random event and have come up with probabilities so small that the human mind cannot even begin to contemplate such numbers. Yet, we accepted this theory by faith."

Jack smiled at my repeated references to accepting things in faith. I think he suspected that I was laying a foundation for a subsequent discussion on "blind faith."

He was correct. But again, I digress.

"Scientists have attempted to replicate the conditions necessary to create life out of nothing but to date have been unsuccessful. So we have Darwin's theory which appears to have flaws and which has not been validated by subsequent fossil finds. Instead, it has been contradicted by subsequent fossil finds, and we have the scientific theory of random generation of life-forms which science is now telling us is statistically highly improbable to the point of being able to be considered impossible. Yet we are still asked to believe in blind faith that these theories explain the origin of life."

Jack conceded that he had accepted Darwin's theory as scientific fact ever since high school and had not given it much thought since then. "Blind faith." He was now having second thoughts about it and scribbled on a notepad which he had brought with him. I sensed a Google search not too far away in Jack's future.

To lighten the mood a little, I told Jack a story, which my children would not find at all surprising. The prospect of Dad telling a story would be taken as a given within my family. Par for the course. I think it is only fair to alert readers to the probability that this will not be the last insertion of one of my anecdotes.

"Even though I am not a pastor or even a lay pastor, over the years, I have occasionally been asked to deliver the message in the Sunday morning service at my local church. The very first time that I did so, in the process of preparation and to ensure that I did not inadvertently offend God or the congregation, I asked my pastor if it was ok to use a joke based on a fictional conversation. Being a very practical person, he assured me that as long as it was within the acceptable boundaries, it is perfectly fine."

"Armed with that assurance, I proceeded to recount the story of a future conversation between a pastor and a leading scientist. The scientist informed the pastor that with the level of scientific advancement, He, God, was no longer necessary. The rest of the conversation progressed something like this:"

"So you don't need God anymore?" asked the scientist.

"No," replied the scientist. "We thank Him for His service, but He can retire now. We can do everything that He can do through science."

The Pastor proceeded to issue a number of challenges which the scientist was able to successfully meet using science.

"Very impressive," said the pastor. "Can you make a man out of sand?"

"Of course," said the scientist. Remember, this is far in the future. The scientist proceeds to scoop up some sand to demonstrate this miraculous scientific achievement when the pastor interrupted him.

"Uh, uh, uh" the pastor admonished. "That is God's sand. You need to use your own." Case closed. Point made. End of discussion.

This story elicited a round of laughter in the church and also drew a healthy chuckle from Jack.

"So, in conclusion, I am not asserting that the first cells could not have been created in the manner that the scientists have asked us to believe—in blind faith. What I am asserting with absolute confidence is that given the complexity of cells of which we are now aware (I resisted the temptation to insert another reference to acceptance by faith as very few of us have ever seen a strand of DNA), it was mathematically impossible for it to have happened by a random event. A simple cell is, in fact, a very very complex mechanism which can only have been created by a process of intelligent design, by an intelligent creator."

"One of my heroes is noted apologist Ravi Zacharias. He has a radio program called "Just a Thought" which airs on a local Christian radio station and which I listen to whenever I can. On one such program, he made this very same point by asserting that if he told someone that a printing press exploded and a dictionary (or encyclopedia) fell out, he would be regarded as crazy."

"In everyday life, if we see a paint stain on the floor, we can accept the fact that open containers of paint may have fallen from a table and resulted in a random, maybe even beautiful, array of colors. We would not, however, accept such an explanation for the existence of a fine and intricate work of art. If there is a painting, there must be a painter."

"I came across a cartoon on the Internet which was satirically demonstrating atheistic thinking. This cartoon had four panels. In the first, a man is admiring a bridge and declares admiration for the great feat of engineering. In the second, he is admiring a sculpture and expresses admiration for the skill and technique of the sculptor who created such a wonderful work of art. In the third, he is admiring a high-powered motorcycle and is marveling at the intricate design. In the last panel, he is in the countryside looking at a river, waterfall, mountains, forests, birds, and animals and comes to the conclusion that it is obvious that none of it was made by anyone."

Jack smiled. Even though he was not yet prepared to admit it, I sensed that he could see the absurdity of the line of thinking which was being illustrated in the cartoon. Man ignores what is obvious but is prepared to accept and believe that which is far-fetched.

"It is also worth noting that even noted atheists are conceding that they cannot explain how the process of initiating life was started. In an interview with Ben Stein for the DocuMovie, *Expelled*, noted atheist and Darwinist Dr. Richard Dawkins can be heard suggesting that intelligent design is a possible explanation. To be fair, his explanation of intelligent design is that life on earth may have been created by an advanced set of aliens, but in any event, he did agree to the likelihood of intelligent design rather than random generation. He has subsequently indicated that he was taken out of context, but having watched the interview, his statements were quite clear to me. Excerpts from this interview are readily available online Jack."

"According to astronomer Dr. Pete Edwards, scientists estimate that there are about one hundred billion galaxies in the visible universe, each of which may have an average of one hundred billion stars. This means that the visible galaxy contains an estimated ten thousand, million, million, million stars. That is ten followed by twenty-two zeros. That means that there are more stars in the visible galaxy than there are grains of sand on the earth. Physicists assert that all of this was created out of nothing in an instant in a massive explosion, a theory now known as the big bang theory. This, of course, begs the questions: How can something be created out of nothing? Even if we accept that something could be created spontaneously out of nothing, what caused it to happen? What caused the big bang?"

"The late Professor Stephen Hawking, also an atheist, was one of the leading proponents of the big bang theory. According to reports carried in the media after his death, he is reported to have said that belief in a God who intervenes in the universe 'to make sure that the good guys win or get rewarded in the next life' was wishful thinking. 'But one can't help asking the question: Why does the universe exist?' he said in 1991. 'I don't know an operational way to give the question or an answer if there is one, a meaning. But it bothers me.'"

"Why then would we accept the assertion that the beauty and complexity that we see around us on earth and beyond are the product of chance? How can we reasonably believe that this complexity and beauty were not specifically, meticulously, and deliberately designed and created? If there is creation, surely there must be a creator.[5]"

I helped myself to a small handful of unsalted cashews and sat back as Jack pondered what I had set before him.

He nodded his head and asked, "You do make a strong case, but how do I know that your scientific assertions are valid?"

"Remember Jack, I am not attempting to convince you on the basis of what I have said today. I can provide additional references and sources, but I do not want you to think that I am providing you with only information to support my viewpoint. I am merely pointing you in the direction of further inquiry, and you can check this yourself. The beauty of the Internet is that an endless amount of information is literally at our fingertips. You will see a lot of articles which support and expand on the points that I have made. You will also see articles which oppose these points, but even after weeding out clearly biased arguments for both viewpoints, I think you will see that there is sufficient scientific weight behind the intelligent design theory."

By now, his wife had brought out a delicious homemade guava cheesecake which we both paused to enjoy.

I sat back and watched him. It was as if I could see the gears turning in his mind as he struggled to come to terms with the arguments that I had put to him.

---

[5] (Romans 1:18–20) "[18] The wrath of God is being revealed from heaven against all the godlessness and wickedness of people, who suppress the truth by their wickedness, [19] since what may be known about God is plain to them, because God has made it plain to them. [20] For since the creation of the world God's invisible qualities—his eternal power and divine nature—have been clearly seen, being understood from what has been made, so that people are without excuse."

"I hate to admit it," he said, "but I can see your point. I am going to research this for myself. There must be more to it than that."

"Of course there is," I replied. "There is a mountain of information which points not only the implausibility of random, chance formation of life but, equally, to the very high degree of probability of intelligent design."

I let that sink in a bit before I transitioned into the next topic that I wanted to discuss with him. Tremendous progress had been made, and I did not want to scare him off by delving into some of the more detailed aspects of this topic. But I was not ready to let him go yet. I had set the bait, he had bitten into the hook, and now I was going to slowly reel him in.

"You will note that I have been focusing on the existence of a creator. An unnamed creator up to this point. This creator is at the center of my belief system. A system that I embrace by faith. As we move forward, if I am able to help you see things differently than how you currently see them, I will take you through my walk of faith and hope to help you understand why I believe that this creator is the Judeo-Christian God. I will seek to explain my faith in God and in His son Jesus Christ. You have been somewhat vocal about Christians following blindly and believing in a God they have never seen and whose existence they cannot prove. At some point, we can have that discussion, but not yet."

"You will also note that I have been emphasizing faith and, in particular, your criticism of it. It seems to me that your sustained focus is somehow linked to the continued existence of this fine food that we have been putting away. Before the food finishes, I would like to discuss 'blind faith' with you, and as before, I ask you to treat it not as a religious discussion, but to give the evidence a fair assessment."

He smiled and could only nod his agreement as his mouth was otherwise occupied at the moment. To be fair to him, he had done exactly as he had undertaken to do. He had given me a fair hearing.

I moved on into my discussion on faith.

"You will recall that the last time we spoke, I used an 'apples and oranges' metaphor to ensure that we both understood precisely what we were discussing. It will be useful to do so again before I get into the substance of the discussion on faith."

"To lay the groundwork for this discussion, let us agree what is meant by 'faith.' In this regard, I have looked at a number of definitions and found the following definitions online. The Merriam-Webster online dictionary includes the following in its definitions of faith:

I. Firm belief in something for which there is no proof
II. Something that is believed especially with strong conviction

There are other definitions which relate to the religious aspect of faith, for example:

I. Belief and trust in and loyalty to God
II. A system of religious beliefs."

"Dictionary.com includes the following definitions which will be seen to be consistent with the ones mentioned above:

I. Confidence or trust in a person or thing
II. Belief that is not based on proof
III. Belief in God."

The Bible itself defines faith as follows in the first verse of Chapter 11 of the book Hebrews:

Now faith is being sure of what we hope for and certain of what we do not see.[6]

"The common underlying factor is that there is a level of confidence or trust which quite often may not be founded on verifiable information."

---

[6] Hebrews 11:1, NIV 1984

"Would you agree Jack that this captures what is meant by faith? That when speaking about Christians' 'blind faith,' what is being referred to or alleged is that Christians are somewhat gullible in believing in things for which there is an insufficient basis for a 'rational, clear-thing person' to conclude that such a belief is valid?"

"Those would not necessarily have been my choice of words Mike, but I guess it does capture the essence of it," he responded with a smile.

"Ok," I continued. "As I did in discussing the creator, I am going to split this discussion into two separate but related parts. What I am going to demonstrate now is that the faith that Christians exercise is not dissimilar to the faith that everyone exercises on a daily basis. In a subsequent discussion, I will demonstrate that far from being without basis, the faith of Christians is actually based on stronger foundations than some of the things that we put our faith in every day. Again, the rationale is to establish a foundation for the religious discussion before actually having a religious discussion. If we cannot agree that the foundation is sound, then there is no point in trying to have a religious discussion. You will note Jack that this is an approach that I will take in discussing a number of points."

He again nodded his agreement with this approach, even as the last piece of cheesecake was disappearing into his mouth. As a gracious host, he had offered it to me, but the two slices that I had already consumed were more than enough.

As sure as night follows day, it was inevitable that more of my stories would make appearances during these discussions. For the most part, those presented as anecdotes reflect sanitized versions of conversations or incidents which actually took place. As I prepared to launch into a couple of illustrative stories, I gently laid the foundations for the approach that I planned to take.

"On a daily basis, we take risks on the strength of blindly believing that we are not facing any risks. Quite often, this belief is based on ignorance. For example, we wake up in the morning, and we fix ourselves breakfast, blindly assuming that the food that we are eating, though not necessarily healthy, at the very least will not be harmful. More and more, we are seeing media reports where some of these foods contain high levels of carcinogenic or other toxic chemicals. In blind faith, we have been eating these for years. How much harm have we done to our bodies over the years as a result of this blind faith in the food packaging and producing companies?"

I know that you have been waiting with bated breath so here comes the first story.

"A few years ago, I ran into a school friend who I had not seen for maybe twenty years or so. In our catching up discussions, he revealed that he was now an engineer at a small regional airline that I used on occasion. It was about the time when there had been some plane crashes worldwide, and safety and maintenance was very topical, so I took the opportunity to ask him to give me the inside scoop on the condition of the planes in the fleet."

He paused a little and said to me, "We have seven planes in the fleet at the moment. Three are relatively new, and there are also four older ones. The newer ones are fine. After the arrival of the newer ones, we took the opportunity to take the older ones out of service one by one, to give them a complete overhaul. When we pulled down the first one, and I saw what condition it was in, I was afraid to fly on the other three! Having said that, we have now completed the overhaul of all four and all are now in good shape."

"Now I am reasonably sure that thousands of people, including me, had flown on those four planes when they may not have been in a condition to inspire safety. Yet in ignorance, we exercised blind faith in the airline and flew on those planes, happily without incident."

"On the topic of air travel," I continued, "how many of us have the capacity to understand the physics which allows a metal cylinder weighing hundreds of tons to defy gravity, fly thousands of feet in the air, and arrive at a destination thousands of miles away? Not many of us. Still yet, without giving it a second thought, we readily engage in air travel, exercising blind faith in the beliefs that the aircrafts are sound, that the pilots are competent and not intoxicated (an assumption which recent media reports have revealed to be not always accurate), and that the maintenance engineer did not have an off-day and neglected to properly tighten an important screw or nut."

I let that sink in for a short while as I sipped from my replenished glass of fruit smoothie before I launched into my next anecdote.

"When we are sick, we go to the doctor who we blindly assume to be competent in the area of our affliction. He prescribes medication which we blindly assume will heal and not harm us. My confidence in medication was shattered years ago when a friend of mine with experience in the pharmaceutical industry told me that there is no such thing as medicine which will specifically target a given ailment only. As he described it, a pharmaceutical drug is a complex chemical compound which has a number of side effects, one of which will treat your ailment. This is evidenced by changes in the way medication is now advertised in the media. It is not unusual to see or read advertisements which devote more time to describing and warning against potentially harmful side effects than is dedicated to describing the positive attributes of the drug."

"One day as I was starting to feel signs of an oncoming bout of the common cold, I went to a drugstore to buy some Vitamin C. We all 'know' that Vitamin C is a good defense against the common cold, right?" I asked as he nodded in agreement.

"I picked up a container of Vitamin C with 'Immune Health*' just below the big 'C' on the label. I thought nothing of the '*' at the time. At some point in the future, when I was again sensing the onset of the 'beast' (common cold), I looked at the back of the container to confirm dosage and noticed the following notation:

'Vitamin C helps the body's cells fight potential oxidative damage and supports the immune system.*'

The asterisk popping up again. About an inch below this statement was another statement in bold capital letters in a box for emphasis. The statement started with an '*.'

"*THESE STATEMENTS HAVE NOT BEEN EVALUATED BY THE FOOD AND DRUG ADMINISTRATION. THIS PRODUCT IS NOT INTENDED TO DIAGNOSE, TREAT, CURE OR PREVENT ANY DISEASE.'"

"Does this mean that in spite of what we all 'know' to be true about Vitamin C, the FDA is apparently casting doubt about this 'fact' that we have accepted by faith, all of our lives? It certainly seems so. Could it be that Vitamin C actually has no positive effect on immune health? Hmm."

I continued with my medical anecdotes.

"As you know Jack, my three children are all asthmatic to varying degrees." Jack would have been aware of the fact my firstborn was considered a chronic asthmatic for the first six years or so of his life, to the point of having had a particular episode at a local hospital which, we were later told, found its way into medical journals.

"As a result, my wife and I became very acquainted with asthma symptoms and treatment. We read in the newspaper about a visiting asthma specialist who was going to be giving a series of talks on the treatment of asthma, and, of course, we decided to attend. Upon arriving, we became aware that the one that we were attending was intended primarily for local general practitioners, and the one for the general public was on the following day. Nevertheless, we stayed and listened. It soon became apparent to us that we were able to answer many of the questions being asked by the attending doctors, doctors to whom members of the public would have been taking their own children for treatment of asthmatic attacks."

"Don't misunderstand me, Jack. I am not knocking these doctors. In fact, I give them great credit for attending this talk in order to update their knowledge base. It just so happens that because of the chronic nature of our son's asthma, we probably had more exposure to a wide spectrum of asthma treatment that many of them did. This does not change the fact, though, that these doctors would have been underprepared to render treatment to patients who accepted their treatment advice in blind faith, assuming that they were getting the correct treatment advice."

"If we can look back at our discussion on intelligent design, millions of people (I resisted the temptation to say including you as I was sure he would figure that out for himself) have accepted an explanation for the existence of the first life-forms, in blind faith. They have accepted it notwithstanding the fact that even scientists who are not religious reluctantly conclude that they cannot explain such processes in the absence of some deliberate action. The scientific method calls for facts to be verified by observation and/or by controlled experiments. Science has been unable to create life. There have been scientific experiments which have been successful in synthesizing some form of organic material, but certainly not anything resembling intelligent life. The fossil record does not verify the Darwinian evolution claims. Microevolution within species has been observed, but not the macroevolution postulated by Darwin. In spite of the conspicuous absence of scientific evidence, scientists still present the theory of evolution as if it was factual. Their belief in this theory is not based on verifiable facts. It is based on faith. Blind faith."

Chapter 4

The food was running out, and I had feared that Jack's attention span would start to wane, but on the back of nice strong cups of Blue Mountain coffee, he soldiered on. By this time, I began to sense that he was genuinely interested in pursuing the discussion. It may well have been primarily an intellectual discussion for him at this point, but if he could be persuaded to reconsider his views on an intellectual level, then half of the battle would have been won.

"Then you are equating normal everyday faith with religious faith?" he asked.

"Actually, I am asserting that for many everyday things which we accept and take for granted, more blind faith is exercised than that exercised by Christians which at least has a basis for this faith. We have not yet discussed this basis, but as we can see from the examples above, some of our daily exercising of blind faith has no reasonable basis."

"When we look, for example, at the odds of commencement of life by random chance, who can reasonably accept that there is a basis for that belief? If you needed a lifesaving operation which the doctors told you had a 0.001%, 1%, or even 10% probability of success, would you take the operation? I would think not. Nevertheless, we have been persuaded to believe that this theory of random chance explains the creation of the first life-forms, a mathematical probability which scientists now tell us is several magnitudes of order more remote than the 0.001% mentioned above."

"At the risk of hearing I told you so Mike," Jack said almost reluctantly, "I must confess that I did some research on this as you suggested, and I will grudgingly agree that there appears to be a stronger argument for intelligent design than for random chance."

At this point, I interrupted him. "Jack," said I, "I need to make a point about research. One of the advantages that we have nowadays is access to never-ending amounts of information on the Internet. This has its advantages but also presents disadvantages. Much of the information on the Internet is false, and in doing research, we need to be sure that we are able to determine which is which. This is not always easy."

Note to the reader:

The vast majority of my research was done via the Internet. Where possible, I checked and cross-checked in an effort to ascertain the accuracy of the information. If I have included information which is inaccurate, please accept the fact that this was not intentional. In fact, I have omitted information which would have been very helpful in making my case but in respect of which I was not confident in its accuracy.

I continued making my point to Jack.

"For example, there is a story which I came across from several sources online which describes a conversation between an atheist professor and a young student by the name of Albert Einstein. Yes, that Albert Einstein. In this conversation, the professor was making a point in class that a loving God could not possibly exist or else He would not have created evil. Young Einstein is reported to have answered him by asking him a series of questions along lines summarized below:

Einstein: 'Does cold exist?'

Professor: 'Of course, cold exists. Step outside now, and you will feel it.'

Einstein: 'On the contrary, cold does not exist. It cannot be measured. What exists and can be measured is heat. What we feel and experience as cold is the absence of heat.'

Einstein: 'Does darkness exist?'

Professor (a little more cautiously): 'Of course, darkness exists.'

Einstein: 'On the contrary, darkness does not exist. It cannot be measured. What exists and can be measured is light. What we experience as darkness is the absence of light.'

Einstein: 'Does evil exist?'

Professor (even more cautiously): 'Of course, evil exists. I have already stated this to be the case.'

No doubt, by now, you see where this is going.

Einstein: 'On the contrary, evil does not exist, at least not in and of itself.'

Einstein is reported to have gone on to assert that what we know as evil is merely the absence of God. In the same way that the concepts of cold and darkness describe the absence of heat and light, similarly, the concept of evil is used to describe the absence of good, morality, and so on, attributes ascribed to God, and is not a 'creation' of God.

Whereas this is an interesting and fascinating exchange involving the young Einstein, the problem is that it appears to exist mainly in folklore, as my scan of the Internet could not find any verification that any such exchange did in fact occur."

"I just wanted to alert you to the probability of you encountering information which can support just about any viewpoint that you wish to support, and as such, the mere existence of this 'information' is not in and of itself a validation of the substance of the information," I concluded.

Note to the reader:

I confess that I have cheated a bit here. I came across this anecdote and was prepared to include it as being attributed to Einstein, but my further research was unable to provide me with a level of confidence as to its genuineness. Nevertheless, I found the approach reportedly taken by "Einstein" to be sufficiently illuminating that I sought to find a way to include it. As such, reader, you can take two things from this sneakily included (but probably fictitious) anecdote. The first is that you need to check your sources and do not believe what you read or hear simply because the information is presented as fact on the Internet or elsewhere. The second is that you should take note of "pseudo" Einstein's argument regarding God creating evil, as this itself is a major stumbling block for unbelievers and believers alike. Whereas this will not provide answers to the question of God and evil, it does address one aspect of it, even though the dialogue appears to have been fictitious.

Now back to Jack.

"Yes, I saw a lot of that, Mike," he said, "articles presenting arguments both for and against, some of which did appear to be somewhat spurious. Having worked my way through many such articles, I will admit that there may be a case for the existence of an intelligent designer behind the creation of the universe and all that is in it."

"Even if I do concede that point, which I am not saying that I am," he was still hedging his bets, "I am still not convinced that this unnamed creator is who you call God. I find it hard to believe some of these so-called miracles which are recorded in the Bible. Are you telling me that you believe in these miracles recorded in the Bible, Mike?"

"As a matter of fact, I do Jack. Not only do I believe in Biblical miracles, but I believe that miracles are still occurring today." I responded to his apparent surprise. We had been at this discussion long enough for him to realize that I would not make a statement like that without good reason. We were not discussing anything which could be regarded as a flight of fancy. Not yet anyway. He waited for me to continue, and I reverted to the trusty definition approach. This time the source was Thesaurus.com.

"Let us consider a miracle to be an extraordinary event in the physical world that surpasses all known human or natural powers and is ascribed to a supernatural cause. We see a number of these in the Bible: raising of the dead, walking on water, healing of the sick, and so on. There have been reports of people being raised from the dead and walking on water in modern times. I do not know what the source of those reports is, and as such, being that I have the same underlying skeptical nature that you do, whereas I do not rule them out as possibilities, I have not necessarily accepted them as being true either."

"Suffice it to say that I have a healthy skepticism, but underneath this skepticism is my belief that there are things taking place in a realm which

I do not, cannot, and may never understand for the rest of my life. I say this to say that I would not try to convince you of those things because I do not know enough about the source of the reports to have confidence in them."

"You will remember a point I made earlier that if you told me that you saw a UFO land and aliens emerge, I would not dismiss it but would believe that you did indeed see it or saw something which you genuinely believed to be a UFO and aliens. That is the same way that I approach our discussion, and I would hope that you would treat anything that I tell you on a similar basis."

"Of course," he said. He had seemed genuinely worried that I was going to tell him that I believed that people were being raised from the dead. This would have been a step further than he was being prepared to take at the moment.

"What I can share with you are four stories (naturally) of occurrences which I believe to have happened as reported, and you can decide for yourself whether or not these constitute modern-day miracles. The first two relate to conversations that I had with two friends who are doctors, both of whom I mentioned earlier. Both of these discussions took place before I became a Christian and helped to reorient my own thinking, eventually playing a part in leading to me taking the step of accepting Jesus as my own personal savior. To my un-Christian mind, both of these stories were beyond belief, and were it not for the respect that I have for the two people recounting these stories, I would have dismissed them as nonsense."

"The third is a story recounted by a friend and business associate of mine with whom I had never previously had a discussion on faith."

"The fourth is a personal experience. Yep, you heard me correctly. I will tell you about something that happened to me."

He was clearly intrigued now.

"The background to the first story was the visit to our city of a well-known international evangelist. I had actually been to hear him speak at a Christian businessmen's luncheon which I attended having been invited by one of the friends from my wife's church. He would later stage a mass open-air outreach meeting at which, among other things, there was the expectation of miraculous healing."

"Yeah, right," I thought skeptically.

"My doctor friend was a member of a team of volunteer doctors who had been recruited to provide support for this Evangelistic event. The story that she told me was stunning. She says that a man (may have been a woman actually, as this detail has faded over the intervening twenty-five plus years) with a leg deformity came forward for healing. One leg was several inches shorter than the other, and as the Evangelist prayed for his leg to be healed, she witnessed the shorter leg start to lengthen to the point where it ended at the same length of the good leg! Let me say it again! She saw the leg grow in a matter of a few seconds! I was speechless!"

"As in the hypothetical case with you and the aliens Jack, because of who was telling me this story, I did not dismiss it outright, as preposterous as it sounded to me at the time. There are people whose integrity I trusted that if I had heard it from them, I would have believed that they thought they saw it but that there was another logical and acceptable explanation which, not being doctors, they may not have known about. Then there were other doctors whom, if they had told me they witnessed a leg grow like that, I would begin to have doubts about their credibility. In her case, as a trusted doctor friend, I was forced to accept that what she saw was exactly what she recounted to me, and this forced me to re-examine my views on what is possible and what is not and to strongly consider, as mentioned above, that there are things happening beyond my capacity to understand or explain them."

"The second story involves another Christian doctor who I also hold in very high esteem. He was an active sportsman and suffered severe damage to his knee in a cycling accident. After a series of surgeries, he was told that he may never be able to walk properly, if at all, on the leg again due to the severity of the damage to his knee. At some point, he received prayer for the healing of his knee and recovered full use of his leg to the point where he again became active in vigorous sorts without any impediment to his leg function and without any pain. Again, because of who was telling me this story, I was forced to believe it."

"The third story was a little different but no less stunning, in some respects, maybe even more so. In the company of two friends from my home church, I took a trip to Miami for a long weekend to play golf and to catch an NFL game. For the record, I am a long-suffering Miami Dolphins fan, and they won that day, so that was a good day for us. Why, you might ask, am I a Miami Dolphins fan? It has to do with the fact that as a non-American, I was introduced to the NFL by friends in Miami in the early to mid-1980s at a time when a young Dan Marino took the Dolphins to the Super Bowl. They had the misfortune to run headfirst into a San Francisco 49ers team led by a rampant Joe Montana. But I digress."

"For one of our golf outings, I invited a business associate who I regard as a friend to join us. For those of you who don't know, golf is not a game. It is a contagious disease in which grown men (and women) subject themselves to endless anguish and frustration and then look forward to doing it again at the next available opportunity. This anguish frequently leads to colorful and loud verbal expressions of this anguish, and at one point, I whispered to my friend that my two companions were members of my church who may feel out of place in such a colorful verbal environment. He duly apologized to them for what he termed 'swearing like a pirate' and then lapsed into unleashing more evidence of piracy as the game progressed and the anguish persisted."

"After the game, we sat together in the clubhouse having an aftergame snack, and I sensed that I should share my faith with him, something which I may not normally have done, but I felt 'led' to do so (remember that phrase, I will come back to it later). I had not gotten very far into my sharing when he interrupted me and said, 'Mike, you don't have to tell me. I have a story to tell you.'"

"He then proceeded to tell us of an incident in his home country where his heavily pregnant wife was robbed on the street by a gunman, who fired a shot into her stomach. As the gunman sped off, she was rushed to a hospital by people from a nearby office building who heard the gunshot and came to her aid."

"By the time he heard what had happened and rushed to the hospital, his wife was in emergency surgery, and he sat and waited for hours, not knowing if his wife and baby were alive or dead and if alive what their future prospects would be. Eventually, the surgeon came out to talk to him and told him that his wife had suffered significant intestinal damage which required removal of a portion of her intestine. She was expected to recover fully and did in due course."

"What about the baby?" he asked anxiously.

In response, the doctor produced a pen and paper and drew a sketch. The bullet entered her abdomen on what he described as a "kill path" toward the baby. It then made a turn and circumnavigated the baby, emerging on the other side. The doctor shook his head and said that he had never ever seen anything like that. As my friend was telling us this story, tears were streaming down his face.

"Mike," he said emotionally, "I know that I do not act like it, but I know that miracles take place. I believe Mike! I believe!"

By now, Jack was utterly captivated. "And the fourth one?" he asked quietly. "What about your own experience?"

"I saved this one for last because, in terms of the scale of the experience, it does not approach any of the first three and may seem like an anticlimax. But at the same time, because it happened to me, whereas I may be 95% confident that the other three incidents really occurred as reported, I am 100% confident in this one because it happened to me."

"Coincidentally, it also involves golf. No, I was not miraculously cured of the disease that is golf even though I suspect that my wife sometimes wishes that I would be. What happened is that I developed very painful tendonitis in my left elbow, which is the golf equivalent of tennis elbow. The result was a very swollen elbow joint after playing golf requiring the application of an ice pack for fifteen minutes or more and resulting in the inability to straighten my arm. I had a permanently bent elbow."

"I visited a leading sports orthopedist who advised me that I should rest it and be prepared for the fact that I may have to give up golf. I quickly decided that in spite of his sterling reputation, he clearly was not as good as he was cracked up to be and sought physiotherapy."

"I did a course of physiotherapy for several weeks which included the application of heat and acupuncture. At the end of this treatment, it had improved significantly, but I still could not straighten the elbow. They recommended a forearm band with a pressure pad which provided support for the tendon and lessened the pain and discomfort, but there was still swelling, albeit not as severely."

"As abandoning golf was out of the question (one cannot simply shrug off a contagious disease after all) I reconciled myself to the fact that I would have to live with the slight swelling and the icing. The forearm band provided sufficient support so that I could not blame my poor golf on the elbow, so on I went more or less happily."

"At that time, I had been a Christian for about ten years or so. I was at home, and my wife had been watching a televangelist on one of the Christian stations. Whereas I have deliberately refrained from calling names in previous stories, in the case, I genuinely cannot remember his name. I was not really watching the program, but it just happened to be on the television in the bedroom where I had been reading in my bed. My attention was caught when I heard him say that there were people watching the broadcast who have been experiencing pains that they have been unable to get rid of and that he was going to pray for healing."

"He encouraged viewers to close their eyes, touch the parts of their bodies where they were experiencing pain, and repeat the prayer that he was about to render. I put down my book, put my right hand on my left elbow, closed my eyes, and repeated the prayer for healing of my elbow, and as soon as I had finished praying, the pain was gone! Never to return!"

"Are you serious Mike?" Jack asked with a look of amazement on his face. "This happened to you?"

"Jack, I give you my word. That is exactly what happened. I am not talking about the pain going away in a couple days. I am not talking about waking up the next morning to find that the pain had gone. I am not talking about the pain gradually reducing over a period of minutes or hours. I am talking about instantly!"

He was stunned by this. The other examples may have been more spectacular, but this one was closer to home. Out of the proverbial horse's mouth. It appeared to me that he was experiencing the same feelings of uncertainty that I experienced when I was told those stories by my two doctor friends.

"What happened next time you played golf?" he asked.

"I played as badly as before but with no pain and no swelling."

"And since then?"

"That was over twelve years ago, and there has been no recurrence."

"Wow!" he said.

"In the interest of full disclosure, I must tell you that I experienced tendonitis in the other elbow a couple years later. I prayed for healing of this one, and nothing happened. Fortunately, physiotherapy was eventually able to correct that one, but that does not take away from what happened with the first one. I can think of no explanation, but that miraculous healing took place."

"In the face of those four stories, I am 100% convinced that miracles still take place. I cannot find any scientific explanation for those events, and therefore, I have no doubt that there was divine intervention in all of those circumstances."

He was frowning a bit now. His reality was being disturbed. Terms of reference being shifted. He was not as confident in his belief system as he was when we started our discussion a few weeks ago.

"So you are saying that those healings that we see on TV are true?" he asked.

"No, I am not saying that," I responded. "Neither am I saying that they are not true. I do not have enough information to be able to render an opinion one way or the other. There may be cases where some of what is portrayed is contrived, but there are cases where it is genuine. All I can say is that I believe that it is possible in most instances. I would like to have been able to confidently say that as leading Christians, if they say these things are true, then we should be able to accept them, but unfortunately, we see that even Christians are subject to human weaknesses and flaws. I do not automatically believe them, but by the same token, I do not automatically disbelieve them."

He thought about this for a while and then said, "Mike, do you not think that there is a scientific explanation for these things? Scientists will tell you that the mind is very powerful and that we are only using a small percentage of our mental capacity. Couldn't it be the case that with your elbow, for example, because you were praying, you somehow tapped into some of this unused mental capacity and, as such, you healed yourself? This seems to me to be a feasible scientific explanation."

"That is a good point, Jack," I replied. "There is, however, an unstated underlying premise in your proposed explanation, which I suggest is incorrect."

This caught him off guard. I do not think that he even contemplated the existence of an underlying premise.

"Underlying premise? What underlying premise?" he asked.

"There is an unstated assumption that if there is a possible scientific explanation, then God could not be involved. Humor me for a minute here, Jack. I have not asked you to agree that God exists, but for the purposes of this discussion, would you agree that if there is a God who created everything, then He would also have created science?"

He thought about it long and hard before conceding that *IF* there is a God, then my assertion would be a logical conclusion.

"Then if He exists and He created science, then what is to say that He would not use the science which He created as the mechanism by which He performs some if not all of His miracles? In my view, the existence of a scientific explanation (even a far-fetched one) is not an argument against the existence of God. It is an argument *FOR* the existence of God."

"Remember that science and Christianity have something in common. They are both subject to ongoing revelation and new discoveries. At any given point in time, lack of scientific knowledge does not render something scientifically impossible. It may simply be that the relevant scientific discovery has not yet been made. For example, it was not scientifically impossible for a man-made device to fly before the Wright brothers and other pioneers made their first flights. Flight was always possible but just had not yet been done. Similarly, the fact that there are things that we do not yet know or understand about the Bible or Christianity does not make them untrue. We just have not yet received that revelation. The absence of evidence is not evidence of absence."

"Mike, you are a horrible man," he said as he feigned anger. "I was happily going along with a fixed set of beliefs, and you have thrown them into complete confusion."

"On the contrary Jack," I responded, "it takes a big man to be able to acknowledge that he may have to rethink his position on anything at all."

"A part of my confusion arises from the fact that I have to admit that some of what you have said makes sense," he said, still not willing to completely accept my assertions. That was fine with me. Baby steps before big ones. He continued, "but it seems to fly in the face of science. Surely scientists are at odds with this?"

It was time for another story.

"I was recently watching television and saw a clip from a sitcom in which the main character was arguing with the pastor at his local church. The character was a science enthusiast and was disputing the validity of religion. His comment was along the lines of science being based on fact and religion being based on faith. If something could not be scientifically proven, it could not be accepted as reality, and therefore, religion was not valid."

"The underlying point here is that by definition, scientists are biased toward empirical evidence. In high school, we were taught the 'scientific method' which involves structured testing and observation in order to investigate the validity of a particular phenomenon. So by definition, if something cannot be proven by the scientific method, then science suggests that the proposed hypothesis or the phenomenon under investigation is false."

"This would suggest that scientists, as a body, should reject any phenomenon which they cannot prove. Religion falls squarely into that category. Since intelligent design has not been 'proven,' then it follows that all scientists should reject the concepts of religion and intelligent design.

Except that this is not so."

"In May and June 2009, the Pew Research Center for the People & Press conducted a survey of scientists who are members of the American Association for the Advancement of Science. The finding confirmed that scientists as a whole are much less religious than the general public. However, it did find that just over half of scientists (fifty-one percent) believe in some form of deity or higher power. Thirty-three percent said they believed in God and eighteen percent, though not specifically believing in God, did confess to believing in some higher power."

"This is not new. Looking back into history, we note the following comments from famous scientists:

- Sir Francis Bacon (1561–1626) is known to have been the founder of the scientific method which I mentioned earlier. In an essay on atheism, he asserted that 'God never wrought miracle to convince atheism, because his ordinary works convince it. It is true, that a little philosophy inclineth man's mind to atheism; but depth in philosophy bringeth men's minds about to religion.' This, from the founder of the scientific method no less!
- Charles Darwin, whose work is the foundation of the theory of evolution, is known to have had his doubts. He is reported to have admitted in a letter a colleague that notwithstanding his views on evolution, it was impossible for him to conceive that this grand universe with our conscious selves arose through chance and that this would be the chief argument for the existence of God. He was not sure if the argument was of real value, but he was uncertain. Though not confessing to belief in a creator, he appears to have agreed that evidence indeed pointed in that direction.

- Albert Einstein though not an actively religious person is reported to have expressed the view that 'Everyone who is seriously committed to the cultivation of science becomes convinced that in all the laws of the universe is manifest a spirit vastly superior to man, and to which we with our powers must feel humble.' Another famous quote of his was 'Science without religion is lame, religion without science is blind.'
- Sir Isaac Newton (1543–1727) is quoted as having said 'What we know is a drop, what we do not know is a vast ocean. The admirable arrangement and harmony of the universe could only have come from the plan of an omniscient and omnipotent being.'
- Francis Collins, director of the Human Genome Project, is a believer in God.
- Earlier I mentioned the views of atheists Stephen Hawking and Richard Dawkins, both of whom, while maintaining their atheistic beliefs, expressed uncertainty as to the actual origins of life.

This is but a small sample of scientists of the past and present who either believe in God, who believe in a superior entity responsible for creation but may not acknowledge this entity as God, or who acknowledge that notwithstanding their strong atheistic views, science cannot explain who or what would have initiated the creation process."

"To be fair," I continued, "there is at least an equally impressive array of scientists who do not believe either in God or any superior being by any other name, do not believe in intelligent design, and often ridicule those who believe entirely by faith, in matters which cannot be proven."

"The delicious irony, of course, is that they cannot prove that there is no God, they cannot disprove intelligent design, and, most significantly, even those who firmly believe in Darwinian evolution cannot explain how the whole process started. So by virtue of their own belief system, they are violating their own belief system."

"What I mean is that they set the bar very high as far as empirical evidence is concerned. They are adamant that their beliefs are based on facts which can be proven, and they denounce faith-based beliefs which cannot be proven or substantiated and then embrace in faith, ideas which are impossible to prove or substantiate and therefore which their own stated belief system should prevent them from accepting."

"I had not thought of that," said Jack. He was smiling now, almost like an excited child who has discovered a new toy. "They are ridiculing the faith of religious people yet putting their own faith in a belief system in which there is not even an explanation. At least for religions, you can debate whether or not the basis for the belief is reasonable, but some of these scientists who are atheists do not even have a reasonable theory to underpin their beliefs."

"Exactly!" I exclaimed, beaming like a proud father who has just seen his son achieve a major milestone. "What further undermines their credibility is that they resort to spurious and weak possibilities to provide the legs for their beliefs to stand on. When challenged on the topic of his lack of belief in intelligent design, for example, one scientist put forward the argument that there was one theory involving crystals mutating and this was the basis for the creation of the first forms of life. Having heard this, it seemed to me to be a case of a cornered scientist trying to defend a weak position. I concede that I am not a scientist, and I do not know much about the crystal mutation theory, and as such, I cannot debate the science of it. However, it still begs the question, 'Even if this theory is correct, what (or who?) caused the crystals to mutate and to create the ultra-complex mechanism that we now know as the 'simple cell'?'"

"I have mentioned comments by Dr. Richard Dawkins. He seems to be of the view that he was ambushed by Ben Stein, but I invite you to search for the interview and arrive at your own conclusions. He states quite clearly that it is possible that life as we know it could *possibly* (this putting forward of an unprovable theory yet again) have been the product of an advanced civilization which was implanted on earth, thus creating our life-forms. So he concedes the possibility of life on earth being the product of intelligent design, just not of a supernatural designer. This advanced civilization, he postulates, would itself have to have been the product of a Darwinian type of evolution. So he has dodged the question of supernatural intelligent design here on earth, but it still begs the question, 'even if his doubtful hypothesis is true, what (or who?) would have initiated the creation of this advanced civilization?'"

"It seems to me that at worst, Dawkins has put forward another very very weak hypothesis which he has no hope of ever proving scientifically and in respect of which there is not even a basis for debating it. At best, he has found a possible explanation which has simply served only to move the locus of the activities of the ultimate creator from here on earth to a galaxy far, far away."

"Remember now that up to this point, we have not been actively debating the existence of the God of the Judeo-Christian Bibles. He has been mentioned only peripherally. We are talking about a body of people of advanced intelligence who deny the existence of intelligent design without having a credible alternative hypothesis. Using the numbers from the Pew Research Center survey, it would seem to me that the fifty-one percent who believe in the existence of God or some other unnamed superior entity are the ones who have employed the scientific method and have arrived at conclusions based on the available evidence. The other forty-nine percent, notwithstanding their scientific bona fides, have eschewed the scientific method and arrived at conclusions not based on where the evidence leads but in spite of where the evidence leads."

"As I was researching the creation vs. evolution debate, I came across a scientific theory referred to as the anthropic principle which posits that the universe is so finely-tuned as to rule out random spontaneous creation, arguing strongly in favor of intelligent design. I came across an article which discusses the theory."

The article was entitled "Is There a God? Arguments for and Against" and was published by Professor Nick Bostrom who as of the date of this writing is listed as Director, Future Humanities Institute, and Director, Governance of Artificial Intelligence Program at Oxford University. At the time the article was published, he was listed at the Department of Philosophy, Yale University.

Bostrom makes the point that before Darwin, one could simply observe the intricacy in the design and functionality of all life-forms and the deist would posit from this, the existence of God. Atheists, on the other hand, could not come up with a feasible explanation for the creation of the world and its inhabitants and focused on philosophical questions such as "why would a Creator exist?" and "If there is a Creator, then why does evil exist? Was evil created by the Creator?"

Even as theologians grappled with these same issues, the advent of the Darwinian theory provided atheists with an explanation for the existence of life-forms on the earth, and they held this explanation to be more rational than that of the existence of a Creator. While creating the appearance that the atheists had triumphed, Bostrom notes that "the atheist has only refuted the deist's argument for God's existence; he has not proved that God does not exist."

He makes the point, however, that given current knowledge, Darwin's theory of evolution cannot explain the statistically improbable (if not impossible) alignment of independent factors (referred to as *anthropic coincidences*) which allow life to exist. The combination of these factors takes place within such narrow margins of error that even miniscule deviations in just one of thousands or millions of such factors would have prevented the existence of life-forms.

Bostrom notes the existence of "a number of (other) parameters that appear (in a similar manner) to have been 'fine-tuned' for the existence of intelligence life. If one uses any natural probability distribution over the possible values that these physical parameters could have, it turns out that there would only be an astronomically small probability that they would have values that permit the evolution of life."

Deists conclude that these statistically impossible anthropic coincidences occur because of God's orderly and deliberate creation of the universe. Atheists, on the other hand, have been unable to provide an alternative explanation, and as result, according to Bostrom, "The balance of evidence seems to have shifted back to favor the deist like it did before Darwin."[7]

I continued. "The article that I mentioned is introductory at best but lays the foundation for the discussion. I must state that Bostrom goes further and outlines other cosmological theories such as the 'inflation theory' and the 'ensemble explanation' which are beyond me but appear to be offering other explanations including the possible existence of multiple universes. I am not even able to comprehend the mysteries of our universe Jack," I said. "The prospect of multiple universes is so far beyond my mind's ability to comprehend that I do not even try."

I fear that I have not done justice to Professor Bostrom's article, and I would encourage the interested reader to search for it online and to personally review it.

"There are strong arguments both for and against the anthropic principle pointing toward intelligent design. In this regard, if I may oversimplify it to make the same point once again, I am not qualified to debate the science, but as was the case with Dawkin's reference of possible intelligent design by a superior alien life-form, the intelligent design argument is not put to rest by even the most elegant of these hypotheses. At best, they simply shift the intelligent design to a different starting point. In fact, some of these hypotheses seem to be suggesting even more complex universes which seem to argue more strongly in favor of intelligent design."

"But I am not a scientist. I can only look at the array of information in front of me and try to arrive at the most logical conclusion suggested by the evidence."

"What I have found interesting is that Christians are sometimes criticized for selecting scriptures which support their particular viewpoint. I will admit that this criticism is not without merit. There are and have been numerous instances of this for reasons varying from insufficient understanding at one end of the spectrum to much more sinister motives at the opposite end, with various shades in between."

---

[7] "Is there a God? Evidence for and Against," Nick Bostrom, www.anthropic-principle/com/preprints/god/god.html

"It seems to me that some scientists are guilty of the very same things. They discount out of hand anything which does not conform to their own points of view. For such scientists, their modus operandi is to structure their 'scientific inquiry' in such a way that they are seeking to disprove rather than establish facts."

"I am not saying that the 'anthropic principle' or the existence of 'anthropic coincidences' verifies the existence of a creator, but what I am saying is that in keeping with the other information that we have for and against spontaneous random generation of life, intelligent design seems to be a far stronger possibility than the various other theories proposed. It must be again noted that none of these theories can disprove the existence of a creator. At best, they shift the origin of the designer's activities to some other point."

"In all of the cases where an argument is put forward in opposition to intelligent design and in favor of random spontaneous generation of life-forms through an evolutionary mechanism, the question can always be asked: 'Even if these theories are true, what (or who?) would have set the process in motion?' To this question, atheists have no answer."

"Strong words, Mike," said Jack, "but I must confess that I can find no flaw in them."

"Jack, if I can use an analogy from the law, there is a legal doctrine known as 'res ipsa loquitur.'"

"I am familiar with it," said Jack. "It is a Latin phrase which translates to 'the thing speaks for itself.'"

"Exactly," I responded. "Put simply, this doctrine holds that one is assumed to be negligent in an occurrence of injury or damage based on the very nature of the accident, even in the absence of direct evidence of an act of negligence. Examples of this include a potted plant falling from a window and injuring someone below, a dead animal carcass found inside a sealed food can, or a surgical instrument left inside a patient following surgery. There may have been no witnesses, but *the thing speaks for itself*. None of these things could have happened without the negligence of someone in control of the items concerned. The evidence points toward a logical conclusion."

"Whereas I am not able to debate the science, I can see where the evidence leads or at least debate that. If scientists can come up with no answer to the question of what initiated life-forms under their various theories and there exists another theory, then *the thing speaks for itself*. The other theory must at least be examined in an unbiased manner and not dismissed outright. Indeed, the very scientific method demands it!"

"I have noticed that a number of the scientists who reject intelligent design are actually taking it one step further. They are not just rejecting intelligent design, they are rejecting a specific intelligent designer. They are rejecting God. The basis for some of these rejections is not so much whether or not there is evidence of intelligent design, but more so, the fact that they find it difficult to believe in God who allows the existence of evil, sickness, suffering, wars, and a host of unpleasant eventualities or who supernaturally intervenes to affect outcomes."

"This is an objection that I can understand. Many of these things are puzzling even for Christians. The fact of the matter is that there are many many things which we do not understand both within and outside religion. Those who argue against Christianity frequently express the view that Christians are gullible and accept whatever their pastors tell them. They argue that there are so many different Christian denominations that they could not all be right."

"There is an element of truth in that line of argument. Are Christians gullible? Some are, some of the time. A system based on faith inherently requires that its adherents accept that which they have no means of proving. In this regard, it is not unreasonable for Christians to accept on face value, that which is taught by their pastors. There are, however, a couple problems with this approach. The first thing is that this assumes that the pastors are always right, which is not the case for a number of possible reasons."

"One reason is that as mentioned above, there are many different Christian denominations (I have seen literature suggesting that there could be thousands) based on the same book, the Bible. For the purposes of this discussion, let us use a figure of one thousand different Christian denominations worldwide. The matter is further complicated by the fact that there are variations in the translations of the Bible, but let us set that aside for now. It is, therefore, reasonable to assume that if there are one thousand different denominations, then at least nine hundred and ninety-nine, if not all one thousand, must be wrong in some material way. This is not an unreasonable argument on the face of it."

"Closer examination, though, reveals that most of the differences arise from differences in doctrinal application but that the central underlying precept of the Risen Christ is present in all but some fringe denominations, which by definition are therefore not Christian at all. For those which are Christian, these differences sometimes relate to interpretations of Scriptural principles which have been debated over the years and which are not likely to be settled during one's lifetime. For the most part, these differences are not major, but there are cases where particular doctrines are preached which are not supported by Scriptures, and in such cases, the blind faith could stray into the area of gullibility."

"So we have identified one area where adherents may be blindly following the teachings of a pastor which may not be entirely correct. Another source of acceptance of wrong doctrine is directly linked to the humanity of the pastors themselves. No one on earth is perfect. As such, we all make mistakes, pastors included. Here again, even when the underlying doctrine of a church is sound, and the pastor himself is sound, the possibility of human error enters the equation."

"There is also another unpleasant source of incorrect information which I will mention in passing here, in the interest of a clear and transparent discussion. It is an unfortunate fact that in most if not all professions, there are those within the profession who do not operate within the legitimate parameters and objectives of the profession. It is not unreasonable to expect, therefore, that there are those who purport to be genuine pastors but whose underlying motive is entirely to obtain financial gain by exploiting trusting believers. They exist, and they do much harm."

"In a lot of respects, the so-called gullible Christians who believe un-Scriptural teaching are no different than non-Christians who seek treatment from 'quack' doctors, legal services from crooked lawyers, or visit fortune-tellers to see what the future holds for them. The same so-called gullibility can be ascribed to those who buy the latest and greatest miracle natural foods or supplements or embrace the latest weight-loss fads, who invest in the latest 'get-rich-quick' schemes or, to bring it closer to home for me, who buy the latest golf clubs guaranteed to improve your golf game and lower your scores."

"This is not a defense of the so-called gullibility of Christians. Rather, it simply serves to illustrate that this gullibility is not a trait which is often taken as a weakness in Christians—it is a trait of humans in general and manifests itself in many ways in everyday life. I would make the point though that whereas in the everyday life cases mentioned above and numerous others which have not been mentioned, we do not always have the means of assessing whether or not we have any reason to believe."

"Christians, on the other hand, have a detailed instruction manual through which they can cross-check everything which a pastor is telling them. In fact, in many churches, the pastors themselves will stress the point that the congregation can and should examine the scriptures themselves to verify the accuracy of the message which has been preached."

I paused to take a sip of freshly squeezed lemonade (or freshly "squozen" as I once heard it described, but that is another story) while Jack reflected on these points.

"So are you saying that Christians are not gullible?" asked Jack.

"What I am saying Jack is that what is being termed gullibility is a feature of humanity rather than a feature of Christianity. In the same way that we exercise blind faith in everyday occurrences, Christians exercise faith in our Christian beliefs. So far, I have been using significant examples of faith such as air travel, doctors' visits, medication, and so on. But we do it on an even more fundamental level. When you drive your car, you do not ever wonder if your brakes are going to work as they should. You proceed on faith. When you sit on a chair, you do not wonder if it is going to collapse. You proceed on faith."

"I remember one occasion when I was at home and sitting down to eat breakfast (this is not about the chair). I proceeded to sweeten my cup of tea with two teaspoons of granulated sugar and took a healthy gulp. Have you ever noticed the strong visual similarity between granulated sugar and salt? Suffice it to say that a mouthful of tea which has been 'sweetened' with two teaspoons of table salt is an experience which I am unlikely to forget. Someone had mistakenly put salt in the sugar bowl, and in blind faith, I assumed that I was adding sugar to my tea."

"So humans can be gullible, or perhaps inherently trusting is a better term to use. Christians have an advantage in that they have an instruction manual, the Bible, as a reference and should, therefore, be able to avoid falling prey to incorrect Scriptural teaching (someone far more clever than I am claims that the word Bible is actually an acronym for Basic Instructions Before Leaving Earth). Being human, however, the common human characteristic sometimes rears its head, and they do not always refer to the instruction manual."

"But even beyond the issue of gullibility is the issue of limitations on our ability to comprehend things which are in evidence around us. Our minds cannot comprehend things which are outside of our normal frames of reference. Take distances, for example. For most of us, our understanding of distance is based on distances on earth. It will take several days to drive across the United States or several hours to fly across. A transatlantic flight from New York to London may take six hours, and a flight from New York to Australia may take more than twenty-four hours. These are vast distances of thousands of miles."

"When we look into the sky in the day and see the sun, we are told and blindly accept the fact that the sun is ninety-three million miles away from the earth. At night we see stars and are told that these stars are so far away that a different unit of measurement had to be created because the units that we used are inadequate. We are told and accept the fact that light travels at a speed of 186,200 miles per second. This means that it would take less than 0.14 seconds for a beam of light to circle the globe. (I am not sure if it is possible for a single beam of light to actually circle the globe, but work with me here. I am just looking at the numbers.) Looking at it in another way, a beam of light could (in theory) circle the earth just about 7.5 times in one second. Our conception of light, therefore, is that it is effectively instantaneous. Our minds cannot readily comprehend the concept of light taking extended periods of time to cover a given distance."

"Yet, we are told that the sun is 93,000,000 miles from the earth and that it takes 8.3 minutes for light to reach us from the sun. We are told these things, and we blindly accept them as factual, just like how we accepted Darwin's evolution theory as factual until scientific advances indicated that it is a flawed premise. Not only do we accept these things as a matter of course, but the possibility that they could be wrong also does not even cross the minds of the majority of people. Were we being gullible when we believe these things? Things that we have no way of verifying?"

"We are told that stars are so far away that conventional units of distance measurement were rendered meaningless and a new unit had to be devised. Accordingly, a unit of measurement called the light-year was created to measure these vast distances. A light-year is the distance that light travels in one year. This is about 5.9 trillion miles. That is 5,900,000,000,000 miles. We are told that earth is in the Milky Way galaxy. We are told that there are more than 100 billion stars in the Milky Way galaxy and that there are more than 100 billion galaxies in the observable universe. We are told that our solar system is located about 25,000 light-years from the center of the Milky Way and 25,000 light-years from its outer rim. Our solar system is said to be approximately halfway between the center and the outer rim of the Milky Way. This would make the Milky Way more than 100,000 light-years in diameter. This is approximately five hundred and ninety thousand trillion miles. We are told these things, and we accept them. We have no way of knowing if these things are true. It is not possible for most of us to even begin to be able to comprehend numbers and distances of these magnitudes, but we accept them as 'scientific facts.' Are we being gullible?"

"While we are on the topic of the universe, we have always been told that the universe has no boundaries. It is supposed to be endless. We have no frame of reference to enable us to understand endless space. Everything on earth has boundaries. But we are told that the universe has no boundaries. And we accept this scientific assertion. Blindly. In faith."

"So I am not saying that Christians are gullible, at least not any more gullible than humanity as a whole. The human nature is to be trusting of anything which seems credible. There are cases where Christians are somewhat naïve and allow themselves to be misled by well-meaning but ill-informed preachers or, worse yet, by scoundrels purporting to be genuine men of God. This could have been avoided if they had taken the necessary steps to ascertain for themselves whether or not what they were being told was biblically sound. In this regard, this is not unlike the otherwise intelligent people who have fallen prey to 'pyramid' or other 'get-rich-quick' schemes. The issue here is not whether people are Christians or not. The issue is that they are people who are prepared to suspend the application of 'common sense' in order to hang on to what may appear to be an unrealistic belief or expectation, whether this is unrealistic investment returns, miracle medicinal cures, or religious convictions."

"Don't misunderstand me, Jack, I am not saying that the astronomers and physicists are wrong about the universe. Like most other people, I suspect, I have accepted that there are things which I do not have enough information to be able to arrive at an accurate position on my own or do not have the capacity to analyze or understand. I have chosen to accept these things, as have you and billions of other people in the world. For some of these things, I have accepted that I do not and never will know the answer, and I am fine with that. I actually believe that the science behind the astronomers' estimates is reasonably sound, and as such, I do not have a basis on which to question it and have accepted it in faith, but I will never know for sure if it is in fact correct."

"The same thought process which has led me to believe these

scientists has led me to conclude that given the intricacies of what we see around us, it is mathematically impossible for the wonders of creation, the universe and everything else, not to have been the product of deliberate design by a far superior being. I happen to believe that this creator is the Judeo-Christian God, the God that I believe in, and if you wish, we can look at why I hold that belief at some point in the future."

That was quite a mouthful, and I paused for a little to take a sip of coffee and to let it sink in before proceeding.

"In our first conversation at lunch a couple weeks ago, you said that if you cannot see it, hear it, taste it, touch it, or smell it, then you do not believe it. I would like to suggest to you that you do not hold that belief in everyday life."

"What do you mean by that?" he asked. I sensed that rather than being suspicious as he was early in our discussions, he was now genuinely interested.

"Have you ever seen a hurricane?" I asked him.

"Of course, I have," he responded. "You remember that we lost a part of our roof in that hurricane a few years ago."

"What does a hurricane look like?" I asked him.

He paused a little to compose his thoughts. He knew what he wanted to say but somehow suspected that there was a flaw which he had not yet identified. My question appeared to be too simplistic.

"There is a lot of wind and rain," he said, "and things being blown around."

"So what does wind look like?" I asked.

Jack smiled as he now saw the flaw in his answer. "Ok," he said. "I cannot see the wind but can see its effect. I will concede that I have never seen a hurricane, but I have experienced more than one."

I continued. "When I asked you a question a while ago, you did not answer immediately. Why not?" I asked him.

"I was thinking about an appropriate response," he said.

"Have you ever seen, heard, tasted, touched, or smelled a thought?" I asked with a smile on my face.

He laughed as said, "Point well taken Mike. There are things which we cannot physically interact with but which we can experience the effects of. There are things that I believe that are real, even though I cannot see, hear, taste, touch, or smell them."

"Exactly!" I said. "Remember that early in our discussion, I asked you to treat our discussions on the same basis that you would treat any other discussion and not hold it to a higher and unreasonable level of agreement than you would for anything else."

He nodded his head in acknowledgment of his agreement to this as a basis for our discussion.

"We have covered some important ground here, and I think this is a good place to stop. Let me just summarize the main things that we have agreed."

"First of all, I think that you have agreed that the probability of the complexity of life being randomly generated is so small as to render it mathematically impossible. This led us to the conclusion that there must have been a creator. I expressed the view that this creator is God but have not yet asked you to accept that premise, just that the evidence strongly suggests that there is a creator."

He nodded.

"Second, we discussed the fact that operating in so-called blind faith is not just a Christian or religious trait but is something that we all do every day without giving it a second thought."

"Third, we discussed miracles, and if not yet completely convinced, I believe that you are at least reconsidering your views on this, in light of what I told you about my own experience and others that have been reliably reported to me."

He nodded.

"Fourth, we looked at the idea of gullibility and agreed that this so-called gullibility, like faith, is a human characteristic which manifests itself both within and outside of Christianity."

"Finally, we agreed that we do not have to be able to see, hear, taste, touch, or smell something for it to be real, but we can experience its effect."

He nodded.

On this note, I closed the discussion so as not to overload him. He needed some time to think about what we had discussed, to do his own research and to decide if he wanted to explore the matter any further. I was pleasantly surprised when he asked me if we could continue our discussion on the following Saturday during a round of golf.

Chapter 5

It should not come as a surprise to you that golf is featured yet again. As I mentioned before, it is, after all, a contagious disease which once it infects you, it is nearly impossible to get rid of, barring a superseding physical infirmity of major proportions.

When I am asked if I am a golfer, I tend to lay no claim to being a golfer but rather an avid golf enthusiast. At my home course on a good day, I will score somewhere between eighty-four and eighty-nine. On an average day, I will score between ninety and ninety-four, and on a bad day, well, that is not worth mentioning. My handicap fluctuates between sixteen and twenty-two but is now at twenty which reflects the current state of my game. This means that on a typical day, I would be expected to score twenty strokes above the par for the course, which, in the case on my home course, is seventy-one. As such, a twenty handicap puts my expected score on a slightly better than average day at ninety-one, which is about right at the moment.

I have had spells where I have scored below ninety on eight out of ten rounds played, and I have had spells where I have scored less than ninety on one out of ten rounds. My lowest score to date has been seventy-nine, a feat which I have been unable to repeat. I have come within sniffing distance on a few occasions, but alas, I have not been able to get below eighty since then, some four years ago now.

There is a particular phenomenon which often manifests itself in amateur golfers which I refer to as DOG golf. DOG here does not refer to the animal but is an acronym for Delusions of Grandeur (as far as I am aware, I coined the phrase "DOG golf" but feel free to use it if you wish). This shows itself in amateurs (particularly men) who insist on playing from the black or blue tees (the ones further back), notwithstanding the fact that they are not competent enough to be playing from those tees. I once had reason to quote a particular scripture to my young church friends (mentioned earlier). Romans 12:3 contains a segment which reads: "Do not think of yourself more highly than you ought." I tend to play from the white tees which are further forward, and even though some of the more accomplished players that I sometimes play with refer to these as the "kiddies tees," it does not bother me. I am not afflicted by DOG.

Anecdotal evidence suggests that a relatively small percentage of active golfers ever score less than ninety much less eighty. Depending on which source you look at, you may see that less than twenty percent (give or take) of active golfers ever score less than ninety. I suppose then I could claim to be in the top twenty percent in the world. Technically that may be true, but the reality is that most of the eighty percent below me are probably only occasional rather than avid golfers, so if we factor those out, that brings me back to where I started. I am a golf enthusiast. The jury is still out as to whether I am a golfer.

Golfers (and golf enthusiasts) do not need a reason to play golf. They just need an opportunity. Or an excuse. Regardless of the circumstances. I once played at an old Irish course in Dublin at the end of September. The temperature was below forty degrees Fahrenheit. And it was raining. Sideways. It was raining sideways. The wind was blowing so hard that the rain was blowing sideways. And we had to walk. In the sideways rain. For five hours. Did we ever think of stopping? Not a chance. There was no lightning, so we were safe, and I was well protected by six layers of clothing. But I digress.

So Jack did not have to twist my arm to get me to play golf, and as agreed, I met Jack at the golf course, and we set off on our adventure. Jack is a better golfer than I am, but the beauty of golf is that people of different skill levels can play together without feeling the need to compete against each other, just enjoying the personal challenge and each other's company.

The course was not crowded, so we were able to play at a leisurely pace without worrying about delaying players behind us or being delayed by people ahead of us. I thought it best to allow him to raise the subject rather than rushing him before he was ready. We played the first two holes (par and double bogey for me, par and bogey for Jack), and as we were heading to the third tee, he initiated the discussion.

"So I spent a fair bit of time researching the science behind the evolution theory and found many strong arguments both for and against. It did seem to me that many of those arguing in favor of Darwinian evolution were actually arguing against biblical creation. What this did was to obscure the question at hand. The question at that point should be, 'Is there a creator or was life the result of random chance?' Instead, much of the debate seems to be arguing against the existence of the God of the Bible."

"I agree with that assessment Jack," I replied. "You will note that in our discussion so far, I have sought to compartmentalize the debate. First, I want to provide you with sufficient information to help you to determine for yourself which is more believable: creation of a complex universe by an intelligent designer or creation of a complex universe by random chance, at odds which any honest scientist should tell you are mathematically impossible."

"I firmly believe in the God of the Bible but will not try to convince you of that. Yet. It would be pointless to try to convince you if you firmly believe in the random chance theory. If you arrive at the conclusion that there must have been a creator, then I will happily take the discussion to the next level and tell you about my God and why I believe in Him."

We teed off on the 390-yard par-4 third hole. Jack hit his driver about 250 yards on the left side of the fairway. I struggle with my driver and hardly use it. I took out my 3 wood and hit a peach of a shot 225 yards just right of center of the fairway. I was twenty-five yards short of Jack but was quite happy with my position. I had 165 yards to the pin which for me would usually be a six-iron shot, but with the wind behind me, I took out the seven iron and hit the ball onto the green, thirty-feet short and a little to the right of the flag. Jack had a relatively simple approach shot which he put just past the hole, giving himself a fifteen-foot putt for birdie.

As we approached the green, Jack said to me, "You know one thing struck me in the arguments being put forward by those opposing the biblical approach. They came up with different theories. I saw the interview with Richard Dawkins that you told me about where he suggested that life on earth may have been initiated by a superior life-form from another planet. This still leaves the questions, where did that life-form come from? And who or what initiated that life-form's existence?"

"The same applies to a number of the other theories. They offer possible explanations for the initiation of life, for example, a burst of energy or lightning which lead to the formation of amino acids and ultimately the first 'simple cell.' Even if we accept these unlikely premises, it still leaves the questions, what was the source of that lightning or burst of energy? Who or what caused it? It seems to me that they have not addressed the issue of whether or not there is a creator but have merely moved the creation process one or more steps back."

"What I find particularly disingenuous is that they dismiss the prospect of a creator as fantasy, but then they offer explanations which themselves are quite far-fetched and devoid of any basis other than wishful speculation," he concluded.

Speaking of "wishful," when watching golf on television, you often hear the commentators saying things like "He is preparing for his birdie putt. This is quite makeable at about thirty feet from the hole." So in theory, I was attempting a birdie putt, but this would represent wishful thinking on my part. In reality, I was hoping to get to within two feet so that I could score four and par the hole. I managed to get the ball to stop about one foot past the hole and accomplished my mission. Jack narrowly missed his birdie putt and also parred the hole.

"I think your analysis is spot-on Jack," I told him as we prepared to take on the 400-yard par 4 into a brisk wind. Usually, I am happy to come away from this hole with a five, but today I mishit a shot from the fairway and ended up with a six to Jack's five.

As we moved on to the fifth tee, Jack said to me, "I think that I am satisfied that there must have been a creator. If the truth be told, I never gave the matter much thought over the years, largely because like the scientists that we spoke about earlier, I had rejected God and this did not allow me to look at the matter rationally. Having said this though, I am still not prepared to accept that this creator is necessarily God."

I don't think he realized it, but by including the word "necessarily" in his statement, he was conceding that in his mind, there was the possibility that the creator that we were speaking of is indeed God. This represented another seemingly small but actually quite significant shift. He has moved from "atheist" to "agnostic" to someone who is considering the possibility that God is real and is the creator of all things. I waited for him to continue.

"The problem that I have," he said, "is that what we know about God comes from the Bible, and I have a lot of doubts about the Bible."

"I understand your position," I replied. "I myself have faced a number of doubts about the Bible over the years, and I may be able to help you come to terms with some of these. Let me remind you though, there are issues where I still have not been able to gain a clear understanding and have accepted the fact that even though I am still searching for answers, I may never be able to find these answers until God himself explains them to me when I am before Him in Heaven."

Jack smiled at this. He had heard me express this a few times in our discussions. And he would probably hear it again.

"In addition, there are topics on which there is no consensus even within Christendom. If any of the issues raised by you fall within this group of topics, I will tell you so. What I will not do is to try to convince you of things that I do not firmly believe myself. Where there are multiple positions, I will also indicate this to you. The end result may be that there may be doubts which you have which I cannot assuage."

"Fair enough," said Jack as we both parred the par 3 fifth hole and headed to the par 5 sixth.

Chapter 6

At more than 500 yards into the wind, the sixth hole is always a challenge for me. Jack hit a good drive, and I hit a decent shot with my 3 wood, but I was forty yards short of Jack. As we proceeded to my ball, he contemplated his first area of doubt.

I prepared to hit my second shot with the 3 wood, and I asked Jack, "What exactly are your concerns about the Bible?" As I waited for a response, I proceeded to slice my 3 wood into the trees on the right side of the fairway. I appear to have mistaken the 3 wood for a "tree" wood (I know that was a really poor attempt at golf humor, but I could not resist it). The rest of the hole was not much better, and I ended up with a two over par 7. Jack missed his par putt and ended with a six.

As we finished up the hole, he responded to my question: "I have quite a few concerns. One of them is that there are so many versions of the Bible now, deviating from the original King James Version. They have changed the scriptures, and Christians still claim that the Bible is inerrant. How can Christians have a book which has so many variations and then claim that it is without error? There are differences, sometimes significant differences, between these different versions, so I cannot understand this claim of inerrancy. That alone shakes the foundation of Christianity as far as I am concerned. The entire belief system is based on a book which has many sometimes conflicting versions. If this is the basis for your belief in God, how can this have any credibility?"

This was quite a mouthful, and as I contemplated my response, I hit my tee shot on the par 4 seventh hole into the water and ended up with a six. Jack scored five, having missed the green with his approach shot.

The issues which he raised were along the lines that I expected, and I had prepared responses to these and other questions which I expected him to ask as we continued.

"Reasonable questions Jack," I said. "The good news is that there are easy answers to these questions. First of all, people of our vintage grew up with the King James Version (KJV) of the Bible. The KJV was commissioned by King James I of England in the early 1600s to conform to the tenets of the Church of England. It became the most popular Bible for close to 500 years but was not, in fact, the original translation. It was not even the original English language translation, earlier ones having been commissioned by King Henry VIII and Queen Elizabeth I. There were also earlier English and non-English translations. The KJV, however, gained such universal acceptance that many people assumed that it was the original Bible translation."

"Oh," he said. "I did not realize that."

As he reflected on this, I continued. "The KJV used language which was common at the time. The prevalence of words such as "thee," "thine," "thou," and the like is merely a reflection of the way that the English language was spoken in England at the time. So dominant was the KJV that even now people still pray using this type of language, as though this was the language of God Himself rather than the common language of the people at that time. As time passed, and the common language changed, it was realized that there was a need to have translations which could be more easily understood by readers. The Bible is complex enough without readers having to decipher the language as well."

"Within the last fifty years or so, several different translations have been done by teams of experts who referred to original texts in Greek and Hebrew and thus were able to correct errors in King James and other earlier translations."

"Did you say errors in the earlier translations?" he asked, almost gleefully. "So you do admit that the Bible contains errors then. What about the claim of inerrancy?" He was sure that he had me cornered now. Even though he was genuinely interested in learning the truth, he was still struggling with the fact that so many long-held beliefs were now being challenged. He now thought that, at last, he was able to recover some lost ground.

I was about to disappoint him. Again.

"Jack, the claim of inerrancy applies only to the original autographs, the original written texts. Errors are introduced as a result of human error in the translation process. Remember also that copies had to be made by hand. As careful as the scribes were, some errors occurred in the copying process as well."

"Translation was particularly tricky as in some cases, the original Hebrew or Greek words or phrases do not have an exact equivalent in English, and as such, some translations provided renditions which were not faithful to the original meanings. Accordingly, when a claim of Biblical inerrancy is made, it does not apply to any of the translations but only to the original manuscripts which are accepted as having been inspired by God."

He gracefully accepted defeat on this point with a smile and nodded for me to continue and continue I did.

"These teams of experts set about compiling new translations in modern-day English. Different philosophies were applied in the translation process, and these differences manifested themselves in some of the differences that you spoke about between the various translations."

"What kind of different philosophies are you talking about?" he asked.

"There are two schools of thought," I responded, "and within each school of thought, there are differences of degree. One school of thought holds that for the translation to be accurate, it must be rendered word for word or as close to word for word as possible. Examples of those which are based on this premise are the King James Version (KJV), New King James Version (NKJV), New American Standard Bible (NASB), English Standard Version (ESV), and the Christian Standard Bible (CSB)."

"The other school of thought holds that the word-for-word approach actually distorts the scriptures in some cases where the language and/or syntax do not exactly correlate. Those who hold this view make changes in the words where they think that such a change, though not an exact translation, better captures the intended meaning of the original writers. Examples of these are the New International Version (NIV) which itself has been updated more than once, the New Revised Standard Version (NRSV), the Contemporary English Version (CEV), and the New Living Translation (NLT). There are others such as the Message which place even more emphasis on readability and the underlying message than on faithful literal translation. To further complicate matters, there are those who hold the view that the deviation from the word-for-word translations represents a deviation from the original scriptures making them less reliable. The opposing view holds that because of the linguistic differences, it is not possible for a word-for-word translation to convey the writers' original intentions."

"There are instances where small changes in the translation can make a huge difference. This has led to some of the misunderstandings and doubts which you have. But it gets even more complex. On top of the challenges posed by differences in the translations, there are different interpretations of the scriptures."

"Isn't that the same thing?" he asked, genuinely puzzled by my statement.

I smiled as I responded. "Your question actually helps to highlight my point regarding difficulties in interpretation. I have used the words 'translation' and 'interpretation,' and in a given context, they could have a similar meaning. In this context, however, they refer to two different things completely."

"Translation is, as discussed above, the examination of the scriptures in their original languages and converting that into other languages, in our case, into English. When I use the word 'interpretation' in this context, I am referring to how the duly translated scriptures are understood by the readers, more specifically, by theologians. What has transpired is that differences in interpretation of the underlying doctrines have led to the formation of different Christian denominations. It is estimated that there are hundreds if not thousands of Christian denominations worldwide, all based on the Bible. These denominations typically differ in their interpretation of one or more Biblical principles or doctrines. In many instances, the differences are not significant, but in some cases, they are quite significant."

"So are you saying that many of these are not true Christians because their belief system is wrong?" he asked.

"Jack, it is not my place to judge anyone," I replied. "Each will have to ensure that they are operating in keeping with God's word and will have to account for their own beliefs and actions."

"Having said that, the Bible does recognize that as humans, we are subject to the frailties of the human condition. In his letter to believers in Rome[8], the apostle Paul encourages his readers not to be concerned about 'disputable matters' (NIV). This leads us to the conclusion that there are matters in the scriptures in respect of which believers will not be in agreement. So the doctrinal differences are not a significant issue as long as the belief in Christ crucified and risen is maintained" (this is, of course, an oversimplification, but I trust that you get the point that I am making here). "Nevertheless, some of these differences are quite significant and see denominations taking widely opposing positions on some of these issues."

"Let me give you a practical example. Most Christians believe that Sunday is the day of corporate worship and attend churches which worship on Sundays. There are, however, some denominations which worship on Saturdays, the Seventh Day Adventists being the most visible of these. Both Sunday and Saturday worshippers are firm in their beliefs and can support their beliefs by referring to their interpretations of specific Scriptures in the Bible. This is an example of differing interpretations leading to doctrinal differences."

---

[8] (Romans 14:1) "Accept him whose faith is weak, without passing judgment on disputable matters."

"Which is correct? I attend church primarily on Sunday, but I respect the rights of the Seventh Day Adventists (and others) to observe Saturday worship. Interestingly enough, the same chapter in Romans mentioned above regarding disputable matters goes on to specifically mention differences of opinion regarding the day of worship and indicates that everyone should do what he or she is convinced in their own minds is the correct thing to do.[9] In fact, if they were to do other than what they thought was right, then that in itself is regarded as being a sin.[10]"

"To be perfectly clear regarding what this scripture is saying, it is not saying that we are free to do whatever we are convinced of in our minds. The context of this is in seeking to determine which of a number of interpretations is correct in God's sight. To the extent that there are strong theological arguments for both Saturday and Sunday worship, then it is incumbent upon believers to prayerfully determine which is correct. We also bear in mind that this is in the passage which opens with an admonishment not to dwell on disputable matters, and as such, we have the confidence that a decision regarding the correct day of worship will not affect our salvation."

He reflected on this for a while as we completed the first nine holes. I had scored forty-three to Jack's forty. Even though I had made some silly mistakes, I was not unhappy with forty-three, but I knew fully well that the second nine holes could be a different story. We stopped at the clubhouse to "recharge our batteries" and headed out to the tenth hole.

I sensed that he was not ready to venture into the depths of a discussion on doctrinal differences just yet. He had what he regarded as more basic hurdles to overcome before he took on doctrinal issues. I suspected that some of these doctrinal differences would pop up later in the natural flow of the conversation.

---

[9] (Romans 14:5–6a) "⁵ One person considers one day more sacred than another; another considers every day alike. Each of them should be fully convinced in their own mind. ⁶ Whoever regards one day as special does so to the Lord."

[10] (James 4:17) "If anyone, then, knows the good they ought to do and doesn't do it, it is sin for them."

"What you have said makes a lot of sense to me Mike. You have helped to clarify a number of what I now realize were misconceptions on my part, but I am still puzzled by some things in the Bible which I cannot reconcile as they do not seem to be realistic for a variety of reasons. Will you give me your thoughts on a few of these?"

"Certainly," I said to him.

This is where the rubber meets the road, and I had no doubt that some of the answers to these could determine whether or not Jack would continue what had now become his quest for the truth or if he would abandon it. I was fully aware of the fact that I had to be very careful. In my own quest, I had been turned off by well-meaning Christians who made statements which meant something to them because of their faith but which were meaningless to someone who did not share their faith. As an example, I remember reading a discussion about the accuracy of the Bible and seeing the argument proposed that the Bible is God's inspired word, so it must be true because God cannot lie. Whereas I agree with this viewpoint, it is not likely to be convincing to someone who does not believe in God. In this regard, I remember the apostle Paul's strategy of amending his approach depending on his audience in order to achieve the desired result of reaching his audience.[11]

"Let's start at the beginning," he said. "The creation story in Genesis says that God created everything in six days and then he rested. I find it hard to believe that this was six twenty-four-hour days, yet I have heard many Christians including pastors take this position. Even though I have committed to being as open-minded as possible, you will not be able to convince me that the earth and everything on it were created in six days. I

---

[11] (1 Corinthians 9: 19–22) "¹⁹ Though I am free and belong to no one, I have made myself a slave to everyone, to win as many as possible. ²⁰ To the Jews I became like a Jew, to win the Jews. To those under the law I became like one under the law (though I myself am not under the law), so as to win those under the law. ²¹ To those not having the law I became like one not having the law (though I am not free from God's law but am under Christ's law) so as to win those not having the law. ²² To the weak I became weak, to win the weak. I have become all things to all people so that by all possible means I might save some."

hear what you are saying about faith, but does faith require us to abandon common sense?"

"Let me address your last point first. Yes, there will be occasions when faith does indeed call for us to abandon 'common sense.' By definition, faith requires complete trust in something or someone, sometimes even in the face of circumstances which suggest that there is no rational reason for this trust. As mentioned earlier, the classic Biblical definition of faith is found in Hebrews 11:1 which reads: 'Now faith is being sure of what we hope for and certain of what we do not see' (NIV84)."

"Having said that, it may surprise you to hear that I actually agree with you on this point," I said as he raised his eyebrows in surprise. I continued. "I have struggled with this for years and cannot come to a position which supports the fact that creation was completed in six twenty-four-hour days."

"But isn't the Bible quite clear on this?" he asked, genuinely interested in hearing my response.

"Actually, I can argue that it is not clear on this." He was even more surprised to hear me say this. Like just about everyone, he was confident that the Bible says that the earth and everything on it were created in six days and that God rested on the seventh day. How could I now be contradicting this well-known fact about the Bible?

"The translations from the original Hebrew state that creation took place in six days, but there is debate among scholars and theologians regarding the meaning of the original texts. The original texts use the Hebrew word *Yom* which has been translated to 'day,' as in a twenty-four-hour day. It is indeed used in this capacity in several places within the Bible. In other places, the same word is used to refer to an extended period rather than a twenty-four-hour day[12], in much the same way as in English we would refer to a time long ago as 'back in the day.'"

"This is one of those points that there has been much scholarly debate

---

[12] (Genesis 2:4) "This *is* the history of the heavens and the earth when they were created, in the *day* that the LORD God made the earth and the heavens" (NKJV).

and lack of consensus on. My own view is that we cannot ignore the science which points to a much longer period for the formation of the earth."

"It is interesting to read the position of noted theologian Dr. Francis Schaeffer, one of the signers of the Chicago Statement on Biblical Inerrancy." In 1978, a group of more than 200 evangelical leaders attended a conference sponsored by the International Council on Biblical Inerrancy, intended to formulate a unified, consistent position on Biblical inerrancy. This position was published as the Chicago Statement on Biblical Inerrancy which, among other things, affirmed that Genesis 1–11 are factual, as is the rest of the book, and also denied that the teachings of Genesis 1–11 are mythical and that scientific hypotheses about earth history or the origin of humanity may be invoked to overthrow what Scripture teaches about creation. One interesting point is that the article was silent on the question of the age of the earth on which there was no unanimity among evangelicals and which was deemed to be beyond the purview of the conference.

In his book, *Genesis in Space and Time*, Dr. Schaeffer expressed this view on the issue:

> *Therefore, we must leave open the exact length of time indicated by day in Genesis. From the study of the word in Hebrew, it is not clear which way it is to be taken; it could be either way. In the light of the word as used in the Bible and the lack of finality of science concerning the problem of dating, in a sense there is no debate because there are no clearly defined terms upon which to debate.*[13]

"So the short answer to your question Jack is that I am not going to try to convince you on this one way or the other. There are eminent and learned theologians who hold and are prepared to defend strong views on both sides of this debate. Regardless of which of the two views you hold, you will be in good company."

---

[13] Genesis in Space and Time, p.57

I could see that he was relieved that I had not tried to convince him on this point in respect of which I think he may have drawn a proverbial "line in the sand," which had I crossed, there may have been no turning back.

"So I am no closer to an answer on this question then," he said.

"Actually I think you are," I responded. "Up to the time that you asked the question, this was a major stumbling block for you. You needed to have this resolved as you were of the impression that if you did not believe in the literal seven days of creation, then there was no way that you could believe anything in the Bible. Now I think that you can accept as I have that there are some things that there are no definite answers to and that is okay. The absence of an answer to some of these questions should not prevent you from believing in the Bible, believing in God. There are eminent highly respected theologians on both sides of this debate—in fact, on three sides of the debate. The first side believes that creation was effected in six twenty-four-hour days. The second side believes that it was not literally twenty-four-hour days and the term day *Yom* was intended to convey periods of indeterminate and differing lengths. The third believes that as there is no way to establish which of the above two is correct, there is no basis for a debate and the matter remains a mystery."

"You say that you have accepted this?" he asked.

"Actually, what I have accepted is that this is one of those things in the Bible which I do not, cannot, and may never ever be able to understand during my lifetime. Given my scientific background in high school and university, I struggled with quite a few things which seemed to defy science and/or logic. This was a major stumbling block for me until I came to the realization that there comes a point where faith demands that I step beyond what I can understand. Once I arrived at the point, it changed my life. I am not suggesting that I now accept and believe everything that I am told. The first thing that I do and would advise you to do is to check what you are told against the word of the Bible to ensure that it lines up. You then have to take the next step to ensure that you have the correct interpretation and when that is accomplished, then this is where faith kicks in."

"But as someone with a background in science, how can you accept things for which there is no scientific explanation?" he asked.

"I can accept them in the same way that I accept things in everyday life for which there is no scientific explanation or substantiation, in the same way that I have accepted for years the fact that Vitamin C is effective in battling the common cold, even though current science is casting doubt on that. There are strong arguments on both sides of that debate as well, and in the same way that I accepted for more than forty years that Darwinian evolution was factual, in spite of the lack of evidence needed to substantiate it. An Internet search will reveal long lists of phenomena and everyday occurrences that science cannot yet explain. This does not mean that they are unexplainable, just that they have not yet been explained, and we learn to live with them in the same way that we accept things for which an explanation exists but which we are incapable of understanding."

"We accept these things in faith, having confidence in the source of the information. We accept a doctor's diagnosis and prescription even though most of us have no way of knowing whether or not the diagnosis is accurate and the prescription will be helpful. We accept them as a result of having faith in the doctor. We step into a passenger airplane not knowing if it is mechanically sound or if the pilots are competent. We accept by faith the premise that the aircraft is sound and the pilots are competent based on the confidence that we have in the airline. Indeed, we have more confidence in an established airline than an unknown airline for this very reason."

"I accept that there are such things as atoms and germs and viruses and bacteria, even though I have never and probably will never be able to personally verify their existence. I accept that there are such things as emotions or thoughts even though there is no way to observe or measure these. I accept these in faith."

"I accept what is written in the Bible because I believe it to be the inspired Word of God. I do recognize that there are aspects of it where there are interpretational challenges and where I may never find the answer in my lifetime, but I can live with that. There are aspects of the Bible which are verifiable in the way that any historical information is verified, and many of these have stood up to the test of historical verification. I am not asking you, Jack, to blindly accept that the Bible is the Word of God just because I say so, or because it says so, but I am asking you to look at it rationally and to determine for yourself whether it can stand up to historical scrutiny."

"What do you mean by that?" Jack asked.

Chapter 7

"I think it would be useful, Jack, for me to outline what the Bible is and, better yet, what it is not. The Bible is quite a remarkable compilation of sixty-six different 'books' written over a period of more than 1,600 years by more than forty different authors. Even though it was written by so many different people over such an extended period, there remains a coherent theme throughout the Bible."

"Is this theme supposed to be the history of mankind?" he asked.

"There is more to it than that Jack. Much of it is history, but not history as recorded by a historian per se. Rather, it represents the history of God's chosen people, the Israelites. As such, it is not intended to chronicle all of the history of all of mankind, but rather to chronicle the history of His chosen people leading to Jesus Christ's second coming and the ultimate salvation of God's people."

"And you believe this?" he asked.

"With all my heart!" I replied enthusiastically.

"Rather than being 'history,' the Bible is described as *historiography* which is a combination of history and theology. All of the books in the Bible have theological underpinning and intent, and history is captured in a manner such that this theological intent can be revealed. This will account for some of the apparent or alleged inconsistencies in the Bible. It was never intended to be a historically accurate book in the sense that historians would regard as accurate. It was intended to describe events which God considered to be significant and which were recorded entirely for the purpose of providing divine guidance for His people."

"Some people challenge the creation story from the point of view of information which is absent. For example, we read that when Cain killed his brother Abel, he fled to the Land of Nod where other people were living. The question is asked: 'Where did these people come from? There is no mention of God creating anyone else?' The fact is that the Bible is silent on this. The further fact is that to the extent that their existence is not material as far as the history of God's chosen people is concerned, then the lack of explanation of this is not a problem. It only becomes a problem for those who hold the view that the Bible is intended to cover every event, which, as I explained, it is not intended so to do."

Jack thought about this for a little while as both parred the tenth hole and moved on to the eleventh hole, a tricky par 3 into the wind, right against the sea. The wind was probably gusting above 20 mph that day, making the tee shot even trickier.

"I have some more questions on the creation story," he said.

"Yes, I thought you might," I replied with a smile.

"The main one is Adam and Eve. I was going to ask you about the inhabitants of the Land of Nod, but I now have a better understanding of the nature of the Bible. Historiography not history, so the people of Nod are not material to the story that the Bible is telling, did I get that right?" he asked.

"You are spot-on Jack," I replied.

"So having established that," he continued, "surely you are not going to try to convince me that the Adam and Eve story is true?"

"As a matter of fact, I am not" I replied, to his surprise. "I am also not going to tell you what my thoughts on the matter are so as not to influence your own views, but I will try to put the matter into perspective for you."

"The fact is that this is another of those topics on which there is no consensus even among Christians. The traditional view is that the story is literally correct as recorded in the Bible. This view has historically enjoyed strong support among Christians even though non-believers find the story to be quite far-fetched. You will appreciate that one's willingness to believe this account will depend on one's point of view. Accordingly, one who believes that God created the earth in all its magnificence would have no problem believing that He has the power to do things which otherwise defy conventional wisdom, no matter how far-fetched they may seem to be. On the other hand, those who do not believe in God would find it difficult to accept anything which they cannot explain."

"There is another viewpoint which is held by some Christians. They hold the view that the Adam and Eve story is intended to be viewed as an allegory and not taken literally. Even within those who hold the allegorical view, there are a number of different theories."

"So are you saying that the Bible could be wrong then?" he asked. "If the opening section is the subject of such significant disagreement, doesn't this render the claims of inerrancy null and void?"

"Remember Jack," I responded, "the claims of inerrancy do not apply to the Bibles that we read today, but only to the original manuscripts. The Adam and Eve story represents a classic example of the differences in interpretation and translation that we discussed earlier. No one knows for sure exactly what Moses was intending to convey when he wrote Genesis which contains the creation story. It has long been taken as if he intended it to be a literal account, but this is now being called into question by some Christian scholars and believers. Which view is correct? I cannot say, but these differing views exist."

My tee shot was carried into the rough by the wind (that's my story, and I am sticking to it), and I ended up with a four on the eleventh hole. Mysteriously, the wind did not affect Jack's shot (must have stopped blowing as he was about to hit), and he was able to par the hole having stopped about a foot short on his twenty-foot birdie putt.

As we completed the par 5 twelfth hole (six for me and five for Jack), he said to me: "As I think about what you have said Mike, a number of my questions can be answered by your historiography explanation. I have often wondered about the absence of any mention of dinosaurs and prehistoric man for which there is fossil evidence, but if as you say the intention is to chronicle specific historical events rather than complete history, then there would be no need to mention them."

"Exactly," I responded. "In the same way, if a historical author was writing about great politicians, there would be no cause to mention great sportsmen unless there was an overlap in that some of these great politicians were also great sportsmen. Great sportsmen were not material to the subject matter of a book on politicians any more than cavemen, dinosaurs, or the origin of the inhabitants of the Land of Nod were material to the theological history of God's chosen people. There was no need to mention them. The absence of evidence is not evidence of absence. The confusion arises when people think that the Bible was intended to track the entire history of mankind. It is in that context that the absence of certain 'significant' pieces of information becomes an issue. Once we realize that the Bible was never intended to cover all bases, then these absences do not pose a problem."

As we moved on to the par 3 thirteenth hole, I could almost see the wheels turning in Jack's brain as he thought about this perspective which was new to him. All of a sudden, more of the questions that he may have had simply disappeared as he correctly anticipated a response along the lines of them not being relevant to God's plan for His people.

He was relatively quiet as we both parred the thirteenth. I hit a ball out of bounds on the fourteenth hole and into the water on the fifteenth ending up with a seven and six, respectively, on those two par 4 holes. Jack fared a bit better scoring five on each hole. Conversation for a while was limited to my disgust at and his commiserations concerning my errant shots, an all-too-familiar occurrence for me I am afraid.

After teeing off on the sixteenth, Jack again asked me to explain what I meant by suggesting that he took a look at the Bible rationally and to determine for himself whether it can stand up to historical scrutiny.

I thought about this for a little before I started my response.

"When examining the accuracy of historical documents, there are a number of factors which have to be taken into consideration." I proceeded to outline the process for Jack, but for the benefit of the reader, I will refer to an article written by Dr. Kenneth Boa of the C.S. Lewis Institute. The article is entitled 'How Accurate Is the Bible?' and was initially published in the Winter 2009 issue of the Institute's publication, *"Knowing & Doing."*

According to Dr. Boa's article, "there are three lines of evidence that support the claim that the Biblical documents are reliable: the bibliographic test, the internal test, and the external test." Boa states that the bibliographic test looks at the quantity, the quality, and the time span of the manuscripts. Using these criteria, Boa asserts that both the Old and New Testaments enjoy far greater manuscript attestation than any other ancient documents.

This can be seen quite clearly, for example, when comparing New Testament manuscripts with other well-known and uncontested ancient writings, a small sample of which will be mentioned below.[14]

There is a gap of some 400 years between the date of writing of Homer's Iliad and the earliest existing manuscript copy (MSS), and there are 1757 existing copies. For Plato's Tetralogies, there is a gap of 1,300 years and 210 manuscripts. For Caesar's Gallic Wars, the gap is 950 years and 251 extant copies. There is a gap of 400 years for Livy's History of Rome of which there are 150 extant copies.

By contrast, there are 5,795 copies of Greek manuscripts of the New Testament with a gap of just forty years. The significance of this small time gap is that there would have been still many people alive who would have knowledge of the incidents recorded in the New Testament manuscripts and who could have disputed them if they were false. It is worth noting that the validity and authenticity of the other ancient documents are seldom, if ever, called into question, yet the authenticity of the New Testament documents is questioned by skeptics.

In addition to the Greek manuscripts, there are also texts which have been translated into other languages. There are in excess of 2,000 Armenian copies with a gap of under 900 years for the earliest copies; 975 Coptic with a gap of under 300 years; over 600 Ethiopian, at least one of

---

[14] Source: The Bibliographical Text Updated, October 1, 2013, Christian Research Institute

which dates back to within 900 years; and more than 10,000 Latin translations, the earliest of which dates back to within 300 years.

To further strengthen the validity of these manuscripts, there are numerous references to the New Testament scriptures in the writings of the early church fathers, some written less than 100 years after the New Testament manuscripts were written. Suffice it to say that if one applies the standard criteria for authenticity of historical documents, there is nothing that even comes close to the New Testament. This has not stopped them from being questioned by skeptics.

My tee shot was pretty decent, leaving me about 120 yards to the pin, set at the back of the green. The wind made the shot a bit trickier, but I still managed to hit my approach shot to within twenty feet of the pin, a genuine shot a birdie, albeit a somewhat difficult one for someone of my (limited) skill level. My putt was dead on track but rolled onto a scuff mark six inches short of the hole which diverted it, and I missed by about half an inch (at least, that's my story, and…). I ended up with a relatively simple par, my eighth of the day. Jack also played steadily, and he too parred the hole.

Not a bad round going so far. If I continued like this, I thought that I might score less than ninety, but I tried not to think about it as such thoughts often lead to disaster. For the record, that comment has nothing to do with superstition, but with concentration. When your mind is distracted, and you are focusing on your score instead of on your shots, that lends itself to errors and errant shots. And high scores. I am sure there is a life lesson in there somewhere. Perhaps, focus on the immediate task and do not be distracted by other objectives? Hmm…

I continued my discussion of the evidence in support of Biblical authenticity by referring to Boa's description of the internal evidence criterion. This looks at what claims the Bible makes about itself. When I mentioned this to Jack, I thought he was going to have a stroke!

"Are you trying to tell me that you are basing your assessment of the validity of the Bible by what the Bible says about itself?" he asked incredulously.

"Yes and no," I replied as he looked at me suspiciously as if all of the credibility that I had built up in our discussions had just been obliterated. But, we had been down this road before, and I sensed that he knew that I had a response to what appeared to be a controversial statement.

So, I responded.

"Remember when we were looking at the number of New Testament documents available and the short period of time between the date of the incidents and the writing of the documents?"

Jack had grasped the pattern of my arguments by now and smiled as he anticipated the direction that I was heading in. "Yes I do," he said.

I continued. "As I mentioned earlier, given the short time gap involved, there would have been many people still alive at the time of writing who would have knowledge of the events that were written about and who would have been able to challenge them if they were not true. We do not see this happening. To the contrary, we see the early church extensively using some of these documents, many of which claim to be eyewitness testimony of the events which had taken place. Had these events been fabricated as is sometimes suggested, it is not likely that such a fabrication would have gone unnoticed."

Jack now laughed heartily. Even though he was giving me a fair chance to present my case, deep down, I think he was still resisting, hoping to find flaws in my arguments, but yet again, he admitted defeat.

"Fair enough Mike. Point taken," he said. "You also mentioned an external test. What is that about?" he asked, now genuinely interested.

Again, I called upon information from Dr. Boa's article. He pointed out that because the Scriptures continually refer to historical events, they are verifiable; their accuracy can be checked by external evidence. There are references to Jesus, John the Baptist, and James by the Jewish historian Flavius Josephus. In addition, there are several other non-biblical references to Jesus, sufficient that there can be no doubt as to His actual existence. A plethora of archaeological discoveries has been able to substantiate the existence of many people and places mentioned in the Bible. All told, there is very strong external evidence which supports the accuracy of Biblical events. In the nineteenth century, some of this was called into doubt by critics, in the face of what was at the time a lack of archaeological findings. However, a multitude of findings in the twentieth century was able to put many of these doubts to rest. This again illustrates the principle that absence of evidence is not evidence of absence.

"So," I said to Jack, "as was in the case of earlier discussions, I am not asking you to accept my assertion based on just what I have said. I am inviting you to use what I have told you as a basis on which you can research this for yourself. I have just barely scratched the surface on this matter. There is so much information available that you will be able to decide whether what I have said is valid or not. I will say, though, that I am confident that you will find that the evidence will leave you with very little doubt as to the historicity of the Bible."

"I will do the research," he said, "but even if I do agree with you on this point, this still cannot convince me that God created the world and that Jesus rose from the dead."

"Quite rightly so," I responded. "One step at a time Jack. I know that you have formulated an opinion over a period of many years. I believe that your particular viewpoint is based on a number of misconceptions, and what I am trying to do is clear up these misconceptions to your satisfaction, and only if that is accomplished, then we can go deeper into the theology. I do believe that we have a fair bit of ground to cover before we get to that point, but would I be correct in saying that arising from our discussions, you have a somewhat different perspective than that which you held before we started our discussions?"

He gave this some thought before agreeing with me, and we completed our round of golf without any further discussions on the matter. I ended with a score of eighty-eight which I was not unhappy with. Jack scored eighty. He pretended to be unhappy about it, but I could see that he was satisfied with his outing.

Chapter 8

Another three weeks passed before I heard from Jack again. In that period he had gone overseas on a business trip, so I know he had been pretty busy. I wondered whether he had had enough of our conversations. If that was the case, I reassured myself that I had covered a fair bit of ground during our discussions and was confident that even if he was not completely convinced, then at least he now had a distinctly different perspective.

I was pleasantly surprised when I received an email from him, inviting me to lunch on the coming Friday. As I had paid for the last one, he even offered to pay for this one. We agreed on a venue and time.

At this point, I was still not sure what his frame of mind was. The invitation to lunch was not in and of itself an indication that he wanted to proceed as we had been having these occasional lunches together for several years now.

For some reason, lunchtime traffic on Friday seems to be a bit heavier than on other days of the week, so even though I left about ten minutes earlier than I usually would have, I still arrived a couple minutes later than the agreed time. The restaurant was closer to Jack's office than mine, and he was waiting there when I arrived.

We exchanged greetings and quickly ordered our meals. He told me about his trip including the round of golf that he played with one of the people that he went to meet, at an exclusive golf club. I must confess that

I was a little envious as that club is not accessible other than to members and their guests. He avoided mentioning his score which led me to believe that the fate that befell him was similar to my experience when I play golf on an unfamiliar course. I typically score ten to fifteen strokes more on an unfamiliar overseas course than I would score on my home course.

But I digress.

As he continued to discuss his trip, he made a very neat segue.

"While I was having dinner at my hotel one night," he said, "I overheard a conversation between some people who were sitting at the table beside me. Based on the nature of the conversation, I was able to conclude that they were Christians."

I smiled and said to him, "So you were listening to the people's conversation? Eavesdropping?"

"No," he said with a chuckle. "The tables were fairly close together. I heard bits and pieces of what they said whether I wanted to or not."

"Anyway, as I was saying before I was rudely interrupted," he continued as I smiled at his playful rebuke, "one of them said something like 'The Lord told me to go and speak to that man about the matter.'" He had deliberately obscured the actual subject matter of the conversation, which in any event was not material to the point he was about to raise.

"Over the years, I have heard Christians ridiculed for saying that God speaks to them, and I must confess that I myself have dismissed such statements as nonsense. What are your thoughts on this?" he asked. "Do you believe that God speaks to you? If so, what does his voice sound like? Morgan Freeman?" he asked with a smile.

"No," I replied. "James Earl Jones." I managed to keep a straight face while I watched his smile start to fade as he tried to figure out if I was serious or not.

I am not sure if he realized what had just transpired. For weeks we had been discussing the possibility of the existence of a creator without focusing on the fact that this creator is necessarily God. Now after a few weeks of contemplation on his own, his opening remark had all but acknowledged the existence of God. His opening remark! This represented a quantum, shift in his mindset. It came on a little more quickly than I had anticipated, and I contemplated whether or not to point this out to him or to "walk boldly through the gate" that he had opened. I believe that one should "never look a proverbial gift horse in the mouth," and so I decided to go with the flow.

This entire contemplation and decision process took place in a fraction of a second. Such is the level of function of a highly tuned mind (for those of you who know me, please allow me some poetic license here). He was still wondering about the James Earl Jones comment, and it was time to put him out of his misery.

"Relax Jack," I assured him. "I do not hear the voice of James Earl Jones talking to me when I pray to God." He seemed to let out a sigh of relief. I have been very open with him so far and have earned his trust. I think that if I told him that I did hear a voice that sounds like James Earl Jones, it would have challenged him severely and upset his equilibrium.

This actually brings me to an interesting point, if I may deviate from my conversation with Jack for a little. Earlier on, we discussed the question of gullibility, Christians being prepared to believe anything. The point was made that this was not merely a characteristic of Christians, but of humans in general and that what may manifest itself as what is called gullibility is actually a reflection of trust and confidence in a person or institution. I mentioned the instances when, out of trust and confidence in my doctor friends, I suspended what I would usually have thought to be possible and embraced the possibility of something happening which I could not comprehend. I may have been considered to have been gullible, but based on the individuals involved, I weighed the options and concluded that my preconceptions needed to be re-examined.

Similarly, in my discussions with Jack, I have been forthright with him and presented him with facts which have enabled him to re-examine some of his preconceptions. He did this out of respect for me and in trust and confidence in my integrity, so much so that he appeared genuinely alarmed when he thought that I might have actually heard a voice sounding like James Earl Jones.

This highlights a challenge that Christians face. In the same way that I believed what my doctor friends told me, and Jack believed what I told him, Christians tend to believe what their pastors tell them. And so should it be. In a perfect world, all pastors would have a clear understanding of the Scriptures, and every message that they convey to their congregations would be in tune with these Scriptures.

Unfortunately, this is not always the case. The Bible is a very complex book, and there are differing interpretations of many Scriptures. Many of these have been the subject of debate among theologians for hundreds of years and may actually never be resolved. So there are cases where what is being preached by well-meaning pastors is not entirely accurate. The matter is further complicated by the fact that not all "pastors" are in fact well-meaning. There are charlatans who purport to be Godly pastors but who are exploiting their congregations and supporters entirely for the purpose of financial gain.

How are Christians supposed to know the difference? Well, we have to remember that we are called to follow the Word of God, not the word of the pastor, unless, of course, the word of the pastor is aligned with the Word of God. In order to be able to discern this difference, as Christians, we should seek to know the Word of God, spending time to prayerfully study the Bible for ourselves and to ensure that what is being preached is in fact consistent with the Word of God.[15] In many churches, the pastors will make this point very strongly from time to time, encouraging their congregants to check what is being said against what is written in the Bible.

But (you must have seen this coming), I digress.

Back to my conversation with Jack.

"Jack," I said, "like you, I have heard many people speak about having conversations with God, just like how you and I are speaking now. I have

---

[15] (Acts 17) "¹¹ Now the Berean Jews were of more noble character than those in Thessalonica, for they received the message with great eagerness and examined the Scriptures every day to see if what Paul said was true. ¹² As a result, many of them believed, as did also a number of prominent Greek women and many Greek men."

never had such conversations with God, and I confess that I have wondered if some of these alleged conversations are in fact genuine. Having said that, it is not my place to judge, and just because I have not experienced it, that does not mean that it cannot and does not happen. I readily admit that there are many people who are a lot more spiritual than I am, and as such, maybe God does speak to them audibly."

"Are you saying that you are not sure that God really speaks audibly to people?" he asked.

"Not at all," I replied. "In fact, I will say that God definitely does speak to people who seek to hear him, but not always in the manner that you think, not necessarily in the Morgan Freeman or James Earl Jones voice."

"So you have heard Him speak to you?" he asked, now very curious.

"I do have a couple of experiences to share with you, but I will get back to those in a little while. Now I think it is better if I gave you a different perspective on what is meant by God speaking to someone. We have already touched on the audible voice. Some people affirm that they actually have conversations with God, conversations involving God speaking and them responding, going back and forth."

Jack's eyebrows raised a bit, and I saw the skepticism on his face.

I continued, "I cannot confirm that particular method as I have not personally had that experience. There are other ways that He speaks to us. The Bible speaks about a 'still small voice.'[16] Some translations refer to it as a 'gentle whisper.'[17] This is another one of those everyday things that we cannot explain but we take for granted."

"Have you ever used the expression 'something told me to…?' For example, you are about to leave home to head to the airport to catch a flight, and just before you leave, 'something tells you to' check to ensure

---

[16] (1 Kings 19:11-12) "¹¹ Then He said, 'Go out, and stand on the mountain before the LORD.' And behold, the LORD passed by, and a great and strong wind tore into the mountains and broke the rocks in pieces before the LORD, *but* the LORD *was* not in the wind; and after the wind an earthquake, *but* the LORD *was* not in the earthquake; ¹² and after the earthquake a fire, *but* the LORD *was* not in the fire; and after the fire a *still small voice*" (NKJV).

[17] For example, NIV

that you have your passport. Sure enough, you had forgotten to pick it up. Or you are searching for your car keys. You search everywhere that you can possibly think that they might be without success. Then 'something tells you' to look in some obscure place that there is no logical reason for you to expect them to be there, and there they are. Or you may have experienced or have heard of people who have experienced something along the following lines: You planned to go to a party or some other function and at the last minute, 'something tells you' not to go. The next day you hear that there was an incident at the party resulting in serious injuries."

"Sometimes we experience premonitions. We have a strong sense that something bad will happen in a given situation (like the party example) and we opt to avoid that situation, and in so doing, we avoid the harm that could have befallen us. Sometimes you are in a crowded place, and you get a feeling that someone is watching you. You are not sure who, and in looking around, you may or may not actually see this person, but you are put into a higher sense of alert. There are occasions when these feelings are just paranoia, but I am sure that you will have had experiences where these feelings have been able to alert you to real dangers, dangers that you had no way of knowing about. I could go on and on about these unexplained feelings that we have and that we accept as a normal part of life," I said.

Jack gave this quite a bit of thought before he responded. "Now that you mention it, Mike, I do use that expression from time to time or a variation of it such as 'my mind told me to....'[18] Are you saying that this was God talking to me?" he asked.

"Before I answer that Jack, let me ask you a few questions."

"Sure," he responded.

"Have you experienced situations where this little voice in your mind alerted you to something that there was no possible way that you could have known? It need not always have been something ominous or sinister.

---

[18] I am not sure how universal this expression is. It is actually used in Jamaica quite a lot, so if it is not familiar to the non-Jamaican reader, please try to grasp the underlying concept rather than the actual phrase.

It may sometimes have been something simple but which, as I said, you had no way of knowing?"

He thought about it for a few seconds and confirmed that he had experienced that on numerous occasions over the years. He recounted incidents when he was driving and "his mind" told him to slow down and he narrowly avoided an accident or a police speed trap.

I continued. "You will agree that there is no way that you can think of that "your mind" could have had knowledge of these things?"

He was very apprehensive because by now, he could see where this was heading. Nevertheless, he conceded that there was no explanation that he could think of.

"So if there was no way that you could possibly have known, but still 'your mind' was able to alert you, would you agree that there must be some mechanism, something external that you do not understand that would have enabled 'your mind' to alert you to the danger?"

He reflected on this one for a while. By now our soup had arrived, and after saying a silent prayer of thanks for the meal, I started on my soup while he was contemplating this point.

After a few minutes, he said, "I suppose you are going to tell me that it was God speaking to me."

"I never said that Jack," I replied, "but let me ask you, can you think of another explanation?"

Apparently, he couldn't, so I let him chew on that for a while. After a few minutes, he said to me, "You said that there are other ways that he speaks to us. You mentioned the 'still small voice.' Are there any other ways that you wanted to share with me?"

"There are a couple others that I wanted to speak about," I replied. "The first may be thought of as a variation of the still small voice. This involves prayer. The second is through the Bible. Let me go back to the still small voice for a while before I go on. When your 'mind tells you to' do something, what does this sound like in your mind? Does it sound like Morgan Freeman?"

He was silent for a while as he reflected on this question. "I have never thought about it before," he said, "but I as I do so now, it comes as a thought in what I guess would be my own voice."

"So," I responded, "a thought on a matter which you agree that you had no explainable way of knowing 'pops' into your mind in your own voice."

He nodded in agreement as he assimilated this revelation.

"File that thought away," I told him. "I will come back to it later. Now regarding the other ways that God speaks to us, let me talk about prayer. We grew up being taught to say grace before meals, giving thanks for the meal which has been provided for us. We were all taught the Lord's prayer,[19] the 'Our Father who art in heaven,' and when we were going to sleep as kids, we were taught to pray 'Gentle Jesus meek and mild, look upon a little child' or 'Now I lay me down to sleep, I pray the Lord, my soul, to keep.'"

"All of those are examples of prayer, but they are prayer in its most basic form. They barely scratch the surface of prayer. When we pray, we should actually be seeking to communicate with God. This involves not only us speaking to Him, but listening to what He has to say to us."

Jack raised his eyebrows at this. I suspect that he had never heard prayer described in this way.

I continued. "This is not something which comes naturally. We, first of all, have to be aware of it and then seek to be attuned to it over time. We have to learn to listen for His voice. We had earlier spoken about the 'still small voice' in your mind which takes the form of your own voice communicating thoughts which could not have been expected to have originated with you. Similarly, when we pray to God, at some point, we need to be quiet and listen to what He has to say to us. As we become attuned to hearing this voice in our minds, His voice, we recognize that

---

[19] (Matthew 6: 9–13) "[9]...Our Father which art in heaven, Hallowed be thy name. [10] Thy kingdom come. Thy will be done in earth, as *it is* in heaven. [11] Give us this day our daily bread. [12] And forgive us our debts, as we forgive our debtors. [13] And lead us not into temptation, but deliver us from evil: For thine is the kingdom, and the power, and the glory, for ever. Amen" (Authorized KJV).

some of the thoughts that we have are not our own, but are actually God speaking to us."

"For example, you may be struggling with a particular problem and are unable to find a solution to it. You spend some time in prayer about it, and as you are praying or waiting for some direction, a thought pops into your mind outlining a solution to your problem. Now, this may be thought of as simply a case of your own mind having solved the problem, and there will be times when that may well be the case. However, as we discussed above, there are times when the 'still small voice' comes up with something that would not otherwise have occurred to you. Looked at in isolation, this may not seem like God is speaking to you, but when we look at it in the context of the 'still small voice' examples above, we recognize that it could indeed be God speaking."

"The other method that I referred to is through the Bible. Usually, when we talk about speaking, we are talking about oral communication, but in the broader sense, the term can be used to describe other forms of communication, such as through the written word. In this regard, we can say that the primary function of the Bible is not just to record the history of God's people just for the sake of recording it, but to provide guidance in keeping with His will. As such, it is quite common for us to refer to the Bible for guidance, and in that regard, we can say that He speaks to us through the Bible."

"How exactly does that work?" Jack asked.

"Well it can work in a number of different ways," I responded. "For example, much of the Old Testament was written not just to record the historical events. Its purpose was to provide encouragement for God's people and to remind them that in spite of the difficulties that they were facing, He was not done with them and that there is a day to look forward to when the faithful will be reunited with Him forever. We are straying into deeper theology here that I do not think it is appropriate for us to get into at this stage of our discussions. Suffice it to say that the point is that the Scriptures were and still are used as a means of encouragement to God's people. Even though as written they were addressing specific issues and circumstances, many of them articulate timeless principles which we can apply to our lives today."

"Can you give me an example of this Mike? A personal example, not something hypothetical or which happened to someone else?" he asked with interest.

"As a matter of fact, I can," I responded. "I have two examples. The first occurred not long after I became a Christian, maybe twenty-four years ago. I was experiencing some difficulties and was really struggling with a particular issue. I was very distressed and depressed, and as I sat on the edge of my bed one night, I cried out to the Lord for relief. Now, please bear in mind that at this point I was a young Christian and did not really know the Bible very well. 'My mind told me' to pick up my Bible, and I opened it to an arbitrary page. As I looked at the page, it turns out that I had opened it to the twelfth chapter of the book of 2 Corinthians written to the church in Corinth by the apostle Paul. In this chapter, Paul is writing about some unspecified (and unknown to this day) distress which he calls a thorn in his flesh. The relevant verses read as follows:

> [7]...*Therefore, in order to keep me from becoming conceited, I was given a thorn in my flesh, a messenger of Satan, to torment me.* [8] *Three times I pleaded with the Lord to take it away from me.* [9] *But he said to me, 'My grace is sufficient for you, for my power is made perfect in weakness...'*[20]

This hit me like a ton of bricks. Here I was moaning and feeling distressed, and 'something told me' to open my Bible and directed me to a passage which speaks of God providing His grace to take me through a difficult situation. He did not say that He would take away the thorn, but that His grace was sufficient to take Paul (and me) through the pain and discomfort of the thorn in the flesh."

I continued, "you might think that this is a coincidence, but that Bible

---

[20] 2 Cor 12:7-9 (NIV)

has over 1800 pages. The odds of instantly arriving at possibly the only scripture (or at least one of a very few) that speaks almost exactly to my situation are minuscule."

Jack was thoroughly captivated by this story. I think that my personal experiences had a more significant effect on him than other examples that I related. Even though they may not seem to be huge, earth-shattering events, they were being reported firsthand by a source that he trusted. I had a couple more to share with him.

"Fast-forward about fifteen years," I said. "By this time, I was a more 'seasoned' Christian but still learning. As I attended church one Sunday morning, I was facing some uncertainty regarding my future. The pastor preached a sermon from a Scripture that, at the time, I did not know very well but would eventually become intimately acquainted with. He was preaching from the 29th chapter of the Old Testament book of Jeremiah. The essence of his message was that God has not forgotten His people, and even though we may not know precisely what He has in mind, He is quite clear on what He is going to do. Jeremiah 29:11 reads as follows:

[11] 'For I know the plans I have for you,' declares the Lord, 'plans to prosper you and not to harm you, plans to give you hope and a future.'

As in the example before, when I was facing uncertainty, the Word of God from the Bible, delivered by His servant the pastor, spoke exactly to my situation and provided me with encouragement which lifted my spirit. But the story does not end there."

"My wife had been teaching Sunday school and had not heard the message. After church, she asked me what the message was about. I told her that I could not remember the scripture (should have written it down, I guess, but I hadn't) but that the line which had impacted me was 'I know the plans I have for you.' I must admit that I was very impressed when, without batting an eyelid, my wife said 'Jeremiah 29:11.' I would eventually come to learn that this was a very popular scripture, but it had not yet registered on me up to that point. There were several scriptures that

I was familiar with and could rattle off at the drop of a hat, but that was not one of them."

"But the story does not end there."

"For us, a typical Sunday afternoon would be that we would prepare Sunday dinner after returning from church, eat, and have a relaxed afternoon. Maybe once over a period of twenty or more years would we decide to take a Sunday evening drive. This is not something that registers on our radar as a rule. However, this particular Sunday, my wife wanted to go for a drive to look at something. So off we went. On our way home, we stopped at a traffic light, and a minivan-type vehicle passed through the intersection, turned, and drove past us. Guess what was spray-painted on the side of this minivan?"

Jack could see where this was going. "Don't tell me it was…"

"Yep," I said. "Jeremiah 29:11."

"I later learned that this vehicle belonged to someone associated with the graduating class of a local Christian high school and that Jeremiah 29:11 was selected as the theme for their graduation ceremonies. But let us look at the series of events."

"First, I heard this scripture for the first time that morning, at a time when I needed to hear it as encouragement. Second, this is probably the only Sunday in a period of twenty plus years that we decided to go for a Sunday evening drive. Third, we drove a particular route which took us to that traffic light. Had we been ten seconds earlier, we would have passed through before the minivan arrived at the intersection. Ten seconds later and it may have been gone by the time we got there, or even if we passed it on the road, I would more than likely have been looking straight ahead and not seen what was written on the side. My understanding is that this was sprayed on the vehicle just for that weekend, so if we had passed it a day or two before or a day or two after, nothing would have been written on the side of it."

"Coincidence? My dearly departed father had a saying which I will paraphrase. I am not sure of the genesis of this saying, so I cannot say for sure whether or not he coined it, but it goes something like this:

When there is an overwhelming incidence of coincidence, it argues overwhelmingly against the coincidence of the incidents.

Or words to that effect."

I pressed on. "We have all seen movies (usually comedies or dramedies) where the main character sees these messages from God, sometimes on billboards, on buses, or on streamers at the back of planes. We treat them as light-hearted departures from reality and don't even give any thought to the possibility of them happening in real life. Yet here it was! I can think of no explanation other than God providing me with words of encouragement at a time when I needed it and reinforced it during the course of the day."

At this point, Jack was lost for words. He sat and stared at me as his food was getting cold. He was really not sure what to make of this story. His logical mind was trying to find an explanation, but he could not.

"Earlier on, you asked me if I have ever had a conversation with God," I continued. "I told you that I have not. What I did not tell you was that I have heard Him speak to me. Twice. The second being a repeat of the first, several years later."

Even in his state of uncertainty following my previous anecdote, I had his full attention now.

"I am not sure how long ago it was, somewhere between fifteen and twenty years I think. I was at home feeling distressed (are you seeing a recurring pattern here?). I had problems at work, my teenagers were, well, being teenagers, and my wife and I had a disagreement, and I was feeling very alone and unloved. I remember lying on the couch in our family room, deeply embedded in a personal pity party, feeling sorry for myself. 'Woe is me,' I thought to myself. 'Nobody loves me,' I thought to myself. At this point, I heard a 'still small voice' in my head say quite clearly, 'I love you.'"

I continued. "Remember now, I have made the case that God speaks to us in various ways and that in many instances (maybe even most, but I do not have sufficient information to be able to state this with confidence), it is in the form of that little voice which sounds like our own voice that pops up in our minds from time to time. As such, I have no doubt that it was God speaking to me at that time. The situation would repeat itself, maybe ten years later. Different challenges, different woes, same pity party. And the same message. The same voice. 'I love you.'"

After staring at me for a while, he returned to his meal. Cold now but still palatable I guess, although he seemed to have lost his appetite somewhat as he did not quite finish it and opted to skip dessert.

He paid the bill, and as we parted company, he said to me, "Well, I did ask you to explain it to me, but I do not think I was prepared for the answer that you gave me."

"What were you expecting?" I asked him.

"To be honest, I am not sure," he replied. "I guess I was expecting you to trot out a list of scriptures where God is reported to have spoken to various people in the Bible."

In my own mind, such a response was one possible course of action, but all throughout our discussions, I have tried to avoid using what the Bible says to validate the Bible. That approach is sometimes seen as circular and lacking credibility by those who reject the Bible. Whereas the arguments may be theologically correct, I thought that they would be unconvincing, and as such, wherever possible, I stayed away from them. This approach is actually scriptural and mirrors the approach of the apostle Paul[21] in tailoring his message to fit his audience. This is not a case of compromising or diluting the message, but rather it is a case of modifying the approach to fit the audience, to reach a given audience by all possible means.

As we walked to our cars, Jack was very pensive but then turned to me. "As usual, Mike, you have left me with much to think about," he said.

---

[21] (1 Cor 9:19–22) "¹⁹ Though I am free and belong to no one, I have made myself a slave to everyone, to win as many as possible. ²⁰ To the Jews I became like a Jew, to win the Jews. To those under the law I became like one under the law (though I myself am not under the law), so as to win those under the law. ²¹ To those not having the law I became like one not having the law (though I am not free from God's law but am under Christ's law), so as to win those not having the law. ²² To the weak I became weak, to win the weak. I have become all things to all people so that *by all possible means* I might save some."

"I am appreciative of the fact that you have not pressured me to continue our discussions and have honored your undertaking to proceed only if I want to. There must have been times when you wondered if you would hear from me, and I confess that there were times when I myself wondered whether I should continue or abandon these discussions. Having said that, I must say that it has been a very worthwhile exercise for me, and I am now committed to seeing it through to whatever conclusion manifests itself. I am still not saying that I am convinced yet, but a number of my strongly held views have been shown to be misconceptions on my part. In hindsight, I am a little embarrassed at some of the things which I have believed and accepted without questioning while teasing you and ridiculing Christians in general."

"I have a lot to think about but would love to get together maybe next weekend if that is ok with you?"

"Fine with me Jack. Why don't you come over to my place on Saturday? We can watch the football game on TV. I will throw a couple steaks on the grill, and we can make an afternoon of it," I replied.

At this point in my fictitious story, I could not decide if the football game was to be an NFL game or real football which our American friends call "soccer." As an aside, the word "soccer" is reported to have originated in England, the home of Association Football which is the formal name of the sport. Association was abbreviated to "socc," and in keeping with popular slang, "er" was added to the end. Similarly, rugby football is known in England as "rugger." In the end, I decided to finesse the issue by leaving the type of football undefined.

But again (say it with me), I digress.

"Sounds like a plan," he said as we parted company.

I headed back to work feeling very encouraged with the direction in which the discussions had proceeded, and I looked forward to our get-together on the following Saturday. The first point of order was to find a couple of New York strip steaks, preferably around 1 ¼ inches thick and between fourteen and sixteen ounces each.

But again… (you know the drill).

Chapter 9

It was a pleasant Saturday afternoon. Slightly overcast, but this was good because it provided cloud cover for the process of grilling the steaks outdoors. Standing over a hot barbecue is enough exposure to heat without having to put up with direct sunshine.

I had indeed found two lovely steaks: one of fourteen ounces and the other sixteen. As a good host, I elected to give Jack the larger of the two while I opted for the "smaller" one. Smaller is, of course, a relative term as a fourteen-ounce steak is a substantial one in its own right. I had seasoned them with my secret seasoning, and they awaited Jack's arrival.

He arrived shortly after the agreed time, and we had a little over an hour before the game. He likes his steak medium, while I prefer mine medium-well, with just a tinge of pink on the inside. I got the grill to the required temperature and put mine on first. After a short head start, his would follow in a few minutes. The trick was to keep them far enough away from the flames to allow the inside to cook without burning the outside and then at the appropriate time, to bring them closer to the fire to sear the outsides. I had by now perfected the art of the steak, and we were both looking forward to them with baited breaths.

Note to the reader: In the interest of full disclosure, I must say that this represents a bit of wishful thinking on my part, but as the book is built around fictitious conversations with my fictitious friend, I took the liberty of embellishing my grilling expertise, just a tad. In the scheme of things, this is not relevant to the essence of the book, so work with me here, please.

My wife had prepared salad and baked potatoes to go along with the steaks, along with garlic bread, and I had blended a homemade fruit punch to accompany the meal. As we stood over the grill eagerly awaiting our steaks, a bread pudding was approaching readiness in the oven, and there was a batch of my special homemade coconut ice cream. By the way, this one is real. I really do make a homemade coconut ice cream along with a delicious vanilla and a chocolate that can stand with any that I have ever tasted.

The steaks did not take long, and the meal was ready about half an hour before the start of the game. This allowed us a little time to have a further chat if that is what Jack wanted to do as I remained determined not to force the issue.

True to his word, he dove in headfirst.

"Mike, I must tell you that I probably would not have had these discussions with anybody else but you. I have known you for nearly fifty years now. We have played marbles, football (the real football), and cricket together over the years. We have partied together and had too much to drink together, and in our younger years, we have gotten up to all sort of shenanigans together. You got married before I did and settled down, but I must say that I have seen a further change in you since you became a Christian. And I have watched you closely."

"I have seen you graciously decline invitations to go out drinking with the boys on a Friday or Saturday night. Not to say that you had a foul mouth, but you did occasionally express yourself colorfully in the past as we all did. I have not heard you do that in well over twenty years now that I think about it, not even when you hit a wayward golf shot, and I can almost see steam coming out of your ears. I think that my teasing you over the years has partly been testing you, prodding you to see if you are genuine or are just like others that I have encountered. But you have put up with it and remained resolute and we have remained friends. I always appreciated the fact that even though you made it clear what your position and beliefs were, you were never condemnatory or judgmental and remained steadfast in your convictions. You did not 'pontificate' and look down on me. I was able to see your Christianity in how you lived your life, not just in what you were saying.[22]"

I was caught off guard and a was more than a little embarrassed by his comments, so I nodded sheepishly and mumbled some incoherent acknowledgment of his kind words.

He continued, "Even though I did not agree with your convictions, I respected them and respected you for sticking with them. Seeing you and interacting with you over the years has changed my perception of Christians, and as a result, when you initiated these discussions, I did not simply shut them down as I would have done with just about anyone else. Now, having had a series of these discussions, I can say that my perspective has been significantly altered, and I believe that I can now approach the topic more rationally. There are still a number of issues that trouble me though."

I nodded in understanding as I silently waited for him to continue.

"One of the major issues that has kept me away from Christianity is what I will call the face of Christianity today. When I look around me, I see a lot of people who profess Christianity, yet other than for an hour or so on Sunday mornings, they are just as immoral as everyone else, in some cases, even more so. Pastors are preying on young women in the congregation. Men and women in the church are involved in adulterous relationships. So-called Christian men are in the bars and nightclubs drunk every weekend instead of being at home with their families. Christian businessmen cheat their customers and exploit their staff. The list goes on and on."

"On an even more basic level, I see a lot of people who go to church, good people, not the immoral ones that I referred to before. Outside of church, there is no sign of Christianity. It seems to me that many of them go to church just for appearances or to make themselves feel religious, but

---

[22] (Matthew 5:16) "[16] In the same way, let your light shine before others, that they may see your good deeds and glorify your Father in heaven."

without really displaying Christianity outside of church. This leads me to think 'why go through the charade?' At least I am being honest with myself by not going to church and not being a hypocrite."

I had been waiting for the 'h' word to pop up. Hypocrite.

He continued. "Having said that, I have been guilty of that myself. My wife has been attending Bible studies with some ladies from the church that she attends from time to time, and I go to church with her and the kids sometimes at Christmas or Easter. It feels like the right thing to do at that time of year."

"The church itself as an institution is also guilty of many nefarious deeds. How many people have been put to death by the church over the years in the name of God? Sexual abuse scandals are rocking entire denominations and are being covered up. The entire institution of Christianity, if I may call it that, is badly tarnished. How can I reasonably be expected to commit myself to such a tainted institution?"

That was quite a mouthful. By now, we had finished eating and still had about ten minutes before the start of the game. This is one of the common objections to Christianity, one which I myself had and therefore could empathize with. Having struggled with these same issues and having overcome them, I felt that I could also address them.

Surprise! Surprise! I had another story!

"Before I specifically address the issues that you have raised," I said, "let me tell you that I had some of these concerns also, both before and after I became a Christian."

"After?" he asked having been surprised by my response.

"Yes," I said, "I will get back to that, for first let me tell you a story."

For some strange reason, he smiled when I mentioned (yet another) story. I ignored the unspoken implications of his smile and forged ahead with my story.

"A man who had been attending a particular church was becoming disenchanted by what he was seeing around him during and after the church service. People were chatting while the pastor was preaching, people were texting and surfing the Internet on their phones, and some were even asleep. On top of this, many did not display what he thought of as Christian characteristics outside of the Sunday morning service. Does this sound familiar to you?"

He smiled in response to that last comment. He could resonate with the sentiment of this man.

I continued. "On the following Sunday, he went to church. He waited until most of the congregation had left and sought a quiet audience with the pastor. He explained his disenchantment to the pastor and told him that he was probably going to stop coming to church as a result. The pastor was sympathetic and understanding but asked the man to come back next Sunday and to see him before the service started."

"As requested, he went to see the pastor just before the start of the service. The pastor gave him a glass full of water. It was filled right to the top. The pastor asked him to walk around the inside of the church with this glass and then come back to him. He was not sure where the pastor was going with this but suspected that it had to do with not spilling the water. He slowly and carefully made his way around the church and was able to return triumphantly to the pastor, not having spilled any of the water. The pastor complimented him on his steadiness and then asked him a question."

"How many people did you see texting on their phones and chatting to each other as you walked around the church?" the pastor asked.

"Well," said he, "all of my attention was focused on the glass of water, so I did not notice anything else that was happening around me."

The pastor smiled and said, "And when you are in church, you should be focusing on God and not on what is taking place around you."

Jack smiled as he grasped the point that I was trying to make. It did not necessarily change his viewpoint in and of itself, but it opened the door to further discussion, so I proceeded.

"One of the things that the Bible calls us to do is to come together regularly as believers so that we can exhort and encourage each other.[23] It is

---

[23] (Matthew 5:24–25) "[24] And let us consider one another in order to stir up love and good

not expected that we are to be perfect. The Bible tells that all have sinned and fall short of the glory of God.[24] We are expected to come together as believers, but our focus should not be on those around us. Our focus should be on God. Even though we are called to come together in fellowship, it is our own personal responsibility to establish a relationship with Christ. We cannot get this through our parents, our kids, our spouses, our pastors, or the people around us in church. It is good to be among them, but at the end of the day, they are not supposed to be the subject of our focus. God is."

"But let's take a look at the people themselves. Not everyone who attends church is necessarily a Christian. As I said earlier, going to church does not make anyone a Christian any more than going to a garage makes someone a car. To be a Christian, one has to have accepted Jesus as his or her personal Lord and Savior. This goes beyond just saying the words. It involves a heart condition. There must be a sincere acceptance of Jesus as Savior."[25]

"The problem is that a lot of people do not know this. Some people genuinely believe that by going to church most Sundays and by participating in various volunteer activities at church, then they are destined for heaven[26] but if they have not established a relationship with Jesus Christ, then they will fall short.[27] In some respects, the problem is worse for peo-

---

works, [25] not forsaking the assembling of ourselves together, as *is* the manner of some, but exhorting *one another…*" (NKJV).

[24] (Romans 3:23–24) "[23] for all have sinned and fall short of the glory of God, [24] and all are justified freely by his grace through the redemption that came by Christ Jesus" (NIV).

[25] (Romans 10: 9–10) "[9] If you declare with your mouth, 'Jesus is Lord,' and *believe in your heart* that God raised him from the dead, you will be saved. [10] For it is with your heart that you believe and are justified, and it is with your mouth that you profess your faith and are saved" (NIV).

[26] (Titus 1:16) "[16] They claim to know God, but by their actions they deny him" (NIV).

[27] (Matthew 7:21–23) "[21] Not everyone who says to me, 'Lord, Lord,' will enter the kingdom of heaven, but only the one who does the will of my Father who is in heaven. [22] Many will say to me on that day, 'Lord, Lord, did we not prophesy in your name and in your name drive out demons and in your name perform many miracles?' [23] Then I will tell them plainly, 'I never knew you. Away from me, you evildoers!'" (NIV)

ple who are not carousing, not involved in adulterous relationships, are good husbands and fathers or wives and mothers, and give generously to the church. If they do not establish their own personal relationship with the Lord, then all that they have done will not be enough."

"This is what I was referring to earlier when I said that I struggled with this both before and after becoming a Christian. In due course, I eventually came to realize that if someone who is attending church is, in fact, a hypocrite, he or she will have to answer to God. As my focus should be on God and not on him or her, it does not affect me. I confess that my imperfect humanity shows itself in that I am sometimes a little irritated by them, but ultimately, it does not have any impact on my relationship with God."

"Having said all of this though, there are people who may appear to attend church just for the sake of attending church, but it is not for us to judge what is in anyone's heart.[28] Our responsibility is to make sure that we are in right standing with God and to address our own faults and flaws rather than to focus on those around us.[29]"

"I have also come to realize that there are people in every church who may fall into the category of 'hypocrite,' or perhaps a better description would be 'apparent hypocrite.' There are also, in every church, those who complain and murmur about these apparent hypocrites. I have concluded that it is not my place or duty to complain. My duty is to do my best and let God do the rest. Where such a problem exists, my responsibility is to conduct myself in such a way that I am able to set a good example

---

[28] (Matthew 7: 1-2) "¹Do not judge, or you too will be judged. ² For in the same way you judge others, you will be judged, and with the measure you use, it will be measured to you" (NIV).

[29] (Matthew 7: 3-5) "³ Why do you look at the speck of sawdust in your brother's eye and pay no attention to the plank in your own eye? ⁴ How can you say to your brother, 'Let me take the speck out of your eye,' when all the time there is a plank in your own eye? ⁵ You hypocrite, first take the plank out of your own eye, and then you will see clearly to remove the speck from your brother's eye" (NIV).

and, hopefully, to have a positive impact on those with whom I come into contact.[30]"

"That sounds reasonable," Jack said. "The more that I think about what we have been discussing Mike, the more that I see where distractions pull our attention away from the matters that we should be focusing on and serve to cloud the issue. When we focus on the distraction, the main issue fades into obscurity as we get sidetracked. It is almost as if the distraction was planned."

"That is an excellent observation Jack," I said, feeling quite pleased that he had picked this up without me explicitly mentioning it. He had also touched on a significant theological point that I did not think he was yet ready to face, so I opted to avoid pursuing this particular point at this time.

"I feel a bit more comfortable now regarding the people in the congregation, but I fear that it could still be a distraction," he said.

"I know what you mean," I responded. "This was my experience too. In fact, it was not until my wife introduced me to the people at the church that she was attending and we became friends that I began to understand what it means to be a Christian. I was able to see what the Christian walk looked like firsthand. It may be that if (when, I thought optimistically) you ever decide to start going back to church, what you need to do is to find a church with people who do not just 'talk the talk,' but also 'walk the walk.' Please bear in mind, though, that even in such an environment, you may find it better than the church that you are accustomed to but that even then, all are subject to the frailties of the human condition and there will be those who present the same distractions that we have been speaking about. It is therefore incumbent on us to remember that we have to focus on God and not on our surroundings."

He smiled as he reflected on what I had just said, and eventually, the smile gave way to a healthy chuckle. "You know Mike, as I listen to your story about your wife introducing you to the people from her church, I

---

[30] (Matthew 5:16) "[16] In the same way, let your light shine before others, that they may see your good deeds and glorify your Father in heaven" (NIV).

now realize that that is probably what my wife has been doing also. She has new friends and has invited some of them over for dinner on a couple of occasions, and we have also visited their homes. She has even been encouraging me to go and play dominoes with a few of the men from the group who have a domino get-together every few weeks."

At this point, I laughed heartily. "It must be in the 'wife DNA' Jack. In my case, my dear wife had me join a group of men to play the board game 'Risk.' It was this interaction that played a significant part in creating a level of comfort and familiarity for me."

He joined me in my laughter and asked, "Would this be the same group of men that you have invited me to play 'Risk' with?"

"The same," I conceded.

"It seems that some of that 'wife DNA' has rubbed off on you Mike," he said in between chuckles. "I must admit though, they are a nice group of guys. Do they all attend your church?"

"As a matter of fact, they don't," I replied. "The composition of the group changes from time to time. There are about twelve of us in total, but on any given night, there are typically five or six. Of the core group, about seven are from my church. Of the other five, three are from other churches, and the other two are friends like you who are not (yet) Christians but who have been friends for a long time and whose company we enjoy."

"When you become a Christian, your life changes, sometimes in big ways and sometimes initially in small ways. One of the changes is that some of the things which used to appeal to you no longer have that appeal, things that you used to do and say, you no longer feel like doing or feel comfortable saying.[31] You how much I love music and I used to like to go to parties. To a very significant degree, that does not appeal to

---

[31] (Titus 3: 3–5) "³ At one time we too were foolish, disobedient, deceived and enslaved by all kinds of passions and pleasures. We lived in malice and envy, being hated and hating one another. ⁴ But when the kindness and love of God our Savior appeared, ⁵ he saved us, not because of righteous things we had done, but because of his mercy. He saved us through the washing of rebirth and renewal by the Holy Spirit" (NIV).

me anymore. I still love music, many kinds of music, but the prospect of going to parties just for the sake of partying has totally fallen off of my radar."

"That has been quite a change," he remarked with a smile.

"It has indeed," I replied. "To the extent that that is the case, a void is left behind. Man still has an inherent need for social interaction. I get that need filled in church, at golf, watching sports with friends, and in playing 'Risk.' Sometimes we play for hours on end. We have been known to organize family outings around us men playing 'Risk' and to play through the night, break for breakfast, and then start again. The beauty of it is that my wife cannot complain. She is the one who encouraged me to start playing with these guys. Two of them are pastors at the church, and others are deacons or other senior men within the church. So an environment is created where men can get together and be involved in entirely wholesome frivolity all night and the wives are comfortable with it. I almost said the wives are happy, but that might have been stretching the point just a tad."

"The point though is that Godly men are involved in fellowship together, and for a newcomer, an opportunity is created for them to see how Christian men operate outside of church and to form their own opinions accordingly."

"I see your point regarding the people in the church," he replied, "but what about the church itself? Would you agree that the image of the church is severely tarnished?"

This one was a bit trickier than all of the other points so far. The fact is that he was perfectly right and I knew that I needed to acknowledge that.

"You are right about that Jack," I said. "I am not going to try to defend the despicable things which have been done by churches over the years. As with the other things that we discussed, however, I am going to try to put them into perspective for you so that it no longer is a stumbling block for you."

He nodded as he waited for me to continue. If he had raised this in our early conversations, he might have expected me to mount a vigorous defense of the conduct of the church, but by now he recognized that that was not my modus operandi.

I continued. "I am going to look at the church from three separate but overlapping viewpoints. The first is the individual church such as any one of the dozens that are within a ten-mile radius of where we are now. The second is the church as a larger countrywide or worldwide institution. Finally, the church as it is referred to in the Bible."

"All three have one thing in common," I said. "Do you care to hazard a guess as to what that thing might be?"

He gave some thought to this. He was sure that this was not as straightforward as it seemed on the face of it, but despite his best efforts, he could not come up with anything but the obvious. After a while, he said, "all are set up for the worship of God." He had deliberately avoided saying "Jesus" in case the trick to the question was one of religious diversity in which case all churches worship God (or god) in some way, shape, or form, but not all worship Jesus.

I smiled as I took note of the care with which he had compiled his answer. "No," I said. "Actually, you are correct, but that is not the answer that I was looking for. They all have more than one thing in common, but I phrased it that way to encourage you to think about it. Good answer by the way, but where I was going with it is down a path which would help to put your concern into perspective. In that regard, the main thing that they have in common is that they all involve people and, as such, are subject to the frailties and failings of all people. The frailties of the human condition that we spoke about a few weeks ago."

"Starting with the last of the three aforementioned, in biblical times, the Jews had synagogues where they assembled, and they also had Temples; the existence and destruction of the Temple in Jerusalem played an integral part in the history of the people of Israel. What they did not have were Christian churches. What the New Testament referred to as 'the church' was the collective name for the body of believers, also known as the Body of Christ.³² Most of these groups of believers met in homes. In due course, they gathered in larger areas which would be analogous to what we call churches now, but the term as used then referred to the people, not the building."

"The term 'church' is also used to describe the entire body of 'Christians' worldwide, regardless of denominational differences, and finally the way in which it is most commonly used is to represent the actual building which formally serves as the place where 'Christians' go to worship. So when I speak to you about going to church, it is the latter that I am referring to."

"Getting back to your concern, let us ignore the Biblical church for the time being. In fact, if you will allow me, I will not address that at all in this particular discussion."

He nodded his agreement.

"Ok," I said as I proceeded. "First, let us consider the individual church. When we typically use the word church, we think of an individual church, not always, but usually."

He nodded.

"By extension, we include the pastor and leaders of the church along with its congregation."

Another nod.

"So what would you say are the factors which would lead you to say that an individual church is tarnished?" I asked him.

He gave it some thought before he replied. "Actually, there are quite a few things," he said. "We have already discussed the people in the congregation, so I don't think we need to rehash that at this point, although I do have some general questions about 'Christians' that I would like to come back to at some point if that is ok with you."

It was my turn to nod, so I nodded.

He paused a little before proceeding as I sensed that he was trying to find the best words with which to express what was in his mind. "The

---

[32] (Colossians 1:18) "¹⁸ And he is the head of the body, the church" (NIV).

main issue would be the way the church is operated. More specifically, the issue would be the conduct of the pastors," he said.

I waited patiently as he organized his thoughts. These discussions were turning out to be harder work than he had initially thought they would be. I was not just giving him answers. Horror of horrors! I was requiring him to think and respond! This of course was deliberate on my part. One does not absorb and internalize information as well when it is given to you as when you are called upon to process it for use. An example which comes to mind is something which happens to me from time to time. I will be giving someone a drive home. As we drive, he or she will give me turn-by-turn directions. I have found that those directions do not always "stick" in my mind and they have to be repeated if I have to go there again. On the other hand, if I am simply given the address, I have to revert to a map. Yes, younger readers, I said map, not GPS, an old-school map. If you are not sure what a map is, Google it. Using the map, I have to figure out the directions, and in so doing, I am more likely to be able to recall these directions in the future.

You know what is coming… but again, I digress.

He continued. "Please do not think that this is an attack on pastors in general, but I am just highlighting issues which have caused me concern over the years. I am not suggesting that all or even most pastors do the things which I am about to mention."

I made a mental note to come back to this point.

"Some of these points have already come up in our discussions. There are pastors who are leading their congregations astray. Some are preaching things which appear to me to be specifically geared toward some personal agenda. Quite often, it involves money. Pastors lay on a guilt trip to squeeze money out of the congregation. There are those who live in mega-mansions and have multiple luxury vehicles and private jets, while some of the congregants struggle to make ends meet. How can they do this with a clear conscience?"

I could see that he was very passionate about this as he continued.

"Then there are the sexual predators. The media has many reports of cases where pastors are preying on the young ladies in the churches, some of whom are married. Even worse are the instances of pastors preying on young boys."

"The examples that I have given relate to what I would call bad pastors. I know that you said we should not judge, but I can find no other way to describe these actions. These are just bad people."

I allowed him to settle before I responded. By now the game had started, but we turned the volume down a bit and continued our discussion, safe in the knowledge that if we missed any action just as it happened, we could catch it on instant replay, or thanks to modern technology, we could rewind it.

"I hear you Jack," I responded, "and I share some of your concerns. There is no doubt that some of the things that you describe are wrong, some even illegal, and those who do those things should face the consequences of their illegal actions. Preying on young boys would fall into that category. Preying on the young ladies may not be illegal but is certainly immoral. Given that such an immoral act is being perpetrated by someone in whom God has entrusted the responsibility for the teaching[33] and the Spiritual well-being of His congregation,[34] it is not only immoral but quite reprehensible. He will have to account to God for his actions and will be severely judged.[35]"

"Now, I am not suggesting that in cases such as sexual misconduct or other criminal acts, the matter should be left to God to handle. Churches have a responsibility to their congregations, and most churches have (or should have) a mechanism in place whereby pastoral misconduct can be

---

[33] (James 3:1) "Not many of you should become teachers, my fellow believers, because you know that we who teach will be judged more strictly."

[34] (1 Peter 5:2-3) "²Be shepherds of God's flock that is under your care, watching over them—not because you must, but because you are willing, as God wants you to be; not pursuing dishonest gain, but eager to serve; ³not lording it over those entrusted to you, but being examples to the flock."

[35] (Matthew 18:6) "⁶If anyone causes one of these little ones—those who believe in me—to stumble, it would be better for them to have a large millstone hung around their neck and to be drowned in the depths of the sea."

addressed, and where necessary, the appropriate authorities should be notified."

"I am glad that you said that your comments are not aimed at pastors in general, but at what I will call 'outliers.' In other words, there is an acknowledgment on your part that in the scheme of things, such pastoral misconduct would be the exception rather than the rule."

He nodded in agreement.

"So here is where we get back to the human element. Churches are populated and administered by people and, as people, are subject to the same human weaknesses as everyone else. I suggest to you, therefore, that the issues that you describe above are reflections or manifestations of humanity rather than the church. These traits of humanity are present in similar fashion in most if not all sectors of civil society."

"You might think that a higher level of moral behavior is expected within the church than outside and you would be correct. We do expect a higher level of morality from Christians, but Christians are not perfect. No one is perfect. The only perfect person died on the cross. Christians are flawed just like everyone else.[36]"

"Let's take a look at everyday life. There are many banks around the world which are well run, profitable, and provide good service to their customers. Every now and again, some sort of wrongdoing comes to light, sometimes leading to huge fines and/or criminal prosecution. We don't condemn all banks and refuse to use them. What we do is exercise more care in selecting the banks that we do business with. This may involve changing banks, or if we are satisfied with the corrective action which seems to have been taken, we will stick with our bank."

"What about government?" I asked. "Government is an institution that is charged with the responsibility of administering the affairs of the country. All over the world, there are instances of wrongdoing, poor government, and even sexual misconduct, similar to that which was described within the church. We see politicians betraying the trust that

---

[36] (Romans 3:23) "[23] for all have sinned and fall short of the glory of God" (NIV).

people have placed in them. Not all politicians, but certainly some do. The police are entrusted with the responsibility of enforcing law and order, but there are instances of police betraying the trust placed in them and committing acts of crime and abuse of power. Not all police. Not most police, but certainly some do. We don't condemn entire governments or all police because of the actions of the few."

"Hospitals are institutions to which we entrust our health care. Most people have pleasant or at least satisfactory experiences at hospitals. But some have terrible experiences ranging from misdiagnosis to bad surgical experiences with doctors to sexual abuse. Not all hospitals. Not most hospitals, but certainly some."

"In all of these cases, we see that institutions and organizations that are set up for good fall prey to the frailties of the human condition and individuals or groups of individuals corrupt the efficacy of the institution, resulting in the institutions being tainted or tarnished."

"Does this sound familiar?" I asked.

Jack smiled and said, "I see where you are going with this, but it sounds to me like you are trying to explain away the bad things that churches do."

"On the contrary Jack," I replied, "what I am trying to do is to establish that the bad things that have caused you to reject churches are not inherently flaws in churches, but flaws in the people involved in the churches. You don't say that you are no longer going to go to a hospital for surgery because you know about corrupt practices at hospitals around the world? You don't decide (or shouldn't) decide to ignore the laws of the land because of the actions of a few corrupt police officers? You don't decide not to send your kids to school because teachers within the school system have been exposed as being involved in a cheating scandal? And you should not abandon hope in churches because of the bad behavior of some pastors."

"Churches have done bad things. There is no getting around that. These things are not a reflection of the institution of the church as a whole but are a reflection of the people in the church. The primary responsibility falls upon the leaders of course, but someone cannot lead if nobody is following, so here again, individuals like you and I have a personal responsibility to ensure that the leadership that we follow is worthy of being followed."

"There are periods in history where the church has committed atrocities, ostensibly in the name of God. In hindsight, we recognize that these acts were not only reprehensible but also entirely contrary to the will of God. The people put their trust in religious leaders and participated in these atrocities. We are again looking at a situation where we can speak about the gullibility of Christians, and again, in hindsight they were gullible. Overly trusting but gullible. As I have said before (and will no doubt say again), this is a human characteristic rather than a Christian characteristic, and we can see similar types of situations happening outside of religion."

"History also records instances of atrocities carried out by oppressive political regimes, many of which were also supported by the people. There are several historical instances where governments have exterminated thousands and even millions of people, in the name of whatever their stated ideology is. The support of the people was in many instances active, but in some cases, it would have been passive. Were these people wicked and evil or just gullible? I suggest to you that they were not inherently evil. Yes, there were some very evil people among them, but the vast majority would largely have been carried along by the popular sentiment of the time."

"This is the same human frailty that is sometimes manifested in religious situations. Most of the countries which carried out these atrocities are now completely different, countries which we are happy to visit. Yes, their past actions were condemned and quite rightly so, but we recognize that those actions were the result of the influence of and misplaced loyalty to some very bad people. Similarly, these past actions of the church were the product of misplaced loyalty in flawed people."

"I say again, I am not trying to make excuses for despicable behavior of the church in the past and even in the present. I am making the strong case that those actions are not reflective of the underlying ethos of the church, and, accordingly, we should not condemn the entire institution of the church. These actions are the product of people within the church at all levels, who are acting contrary to the will and purpose of the church and are thereby corrupting the church."

"You make a strong case Mike," said Jack, "but what about situations which are condoned by the church? We see and read reports of such abuses all too often these days."

"I agree with you 100% Jack," I responded, "and my assertion has not changed. If these actions are being condoned by the church, then the church is in error and acting contrary to the will of God. There can be no doubt about that. I think that you will find that in many of the cases which we are seeing reported these days, the church is, in fact, taking action. The problem seems to be that in some instances, the abuses had been ongoing for many years and were not properly dealt with."

"Before I leave the topic of churches, you had some concerns about pastors always asking for money. I understand the concern, particularly when the call for money is coming from mega-rich pastors. I am not judging them for this as some of them earn substantial amounts from the sale of books which they have written and other business ventures. There is absolutely nothing wrong, in my view, with a pastor who earns money from his income-earning activities being able to spend it as he sees fit. The underlying question would be how they handle their earnings in the wider sense. It would be hard to support a pastor who is earning millions of dollars and using it to build his own fortune while not sowing into the Kingdom of God. There is one well-known pastor who wrote a best-selling book and only kept ten percent of the profits, the other ninety percent being plowed into the work of the church."

"On a more fundamental level, churches do a lot of work for their congregants and community and are also engaged in various forms of outreach activity. The funding for this has to come from somewhere, and it is entirely Scriptural to expect these activities to be funded by the congregants of the church. From that point of view, it is entirely in order for the pastors to exhort the congregation to provide support for the churches' activities."

I know that this is always a sore point with non-Christians, many of whom view churches as moneymaking enterprises. This perception is unfortunately aided and abetted by the fact that there are, in fact, "churches" that do operate on that basis. As discussed above, though, these should not be considered as true Christian churches. I could see that Jack was not entirely convinced, but I was confident that after a period of reflection, he would accept it even if not agreeing entirely with it.

Chapter 10

The game had started to show signs of excitement, and we suspended our discussion so that we could enjoy it. At the half-time interval, Jack said to me, "We have covered a lot of ground today, but there is something else that I would like to hear your thoughts on. Do you have the time for us to continue after the game?"

"Certainly," I responded as we refreshed ourselves and settled in to watch the second half.

The game came to an exciting climax with the team that we both supported eking out a victory in the closing minutes. We spent a few minutes discussing some of the outstanding plays of the game and the prospects of our team winning the championship this season, after an extended period in the wilderness. We then retired to the back patio to enjoy some cold drinks and to continue our conversation. As usual, I allowed him to start when he was ready.

"You know Mike," he said, "I have had a lot of misconceptions which, I must admit, you have been able to provide me with new perspectives on. As I have reflected on that, it occurs to me that my conception of Christians seems to be very wrong. I have always thought of Christians as being 'holier than thou' 'goody-two-shoes' type of people who purport to never do anything wrong and live boring, restricted lives, with the women wearing long dresses and wearing no makeup and all told—the lifestyle is quite unattractive to me. I have heard televangelists speaking to large audiences and making pronouncements along the lines that everything is going to be great for them and that they will all be blessed. The impression is given that Christianity is a guarantee of success and prosperity and that all will be well. Christians will not have any problems that they can overcome. After all, doesn't the Bible say that the Lord will not give you any more than you can bear?"

He went on a bit further and outlined more of the perceptions that he had about Christians and Christianity. He seemed to want to get this off of his chest, so I allowed him to continue uninterrupted, mentally making a note of the points that I needed to address. After he had finished speaking, I proceeded to answer him.

"There is a matter which may have come up in our earlier discussions that I want to get back to here, in order to lay the foundation for parts of my response. This is the issue of the correct application of Scripture or, rather, the effect of the incorrect application of Scripture. I want to approach this from two points of view. The first relates to the difficult task of interpreting many Scriptures. Such difficulties result in differing and sometimes incorrect interpretations, both of which give rise to different perceptions and application of Scripture to everyday lives. You will agree that if one is basing actions or perceptions on incorrect Scriptures, for example, then it follows that the perceptions or actions will not be correct from a Scriptural point of view."

I paused briefly to allow this to sink in and he nodded in agreement.

I continued. "There are also situations in which Scripture is applied in a way which is thought to be correct, but in respect of which, there are different positions held by different churches or denominations. At times, it may be difficult to determine which of these interpretations is correct. Where these differing interpretations are not contrary to the core doctrine of Christianity—that being Christ crucified and risen—the differences are not going to affect ones' salvation. In fact, you will recall that I told you of the apostle Paul's instruction to the believers in Rome to not quarrel over disputable matters.[37] However, these differences can

---

[37] (Romans 14:1) "Accept the one whose faith is weak, without quarreling over disputable matters" (NIV).

affect how people perceive Christians. They can even affect how some Christians perceive other Christians."

"One of the points that you raised relates to how Christians look and dress. Sometimes you see a modestly dressed lady with a modest hairstyle and conclude that she looks like a Christian. There are Scriptures in the Bible which speak about how ladies should dress and adorn themselves or, better yet, not adorn themselves.[38] Such Scriptures are interpreted in a number of different ways."

"One school of thought is that they are to be interpreted literally and should be applied literally even these days. Adherents to that interpretation will dress modestly, in the manner which you refer to as the 'Christian' look or style. The other school of thought is that those Scriptures should be interpreted according to the context of the church(es) and to which they were written, taking into account the social and cultural environment obtaining at the time and the specific issue that the writer of that Scripture was seeking to address. Supporters of that interpretation do not see the need to adhere to any particular standard or style of dress, other than to ensure that they are not dressing in a way which encourages sensual thoughts."

"Which one is right? I have my views on it, and these views are reflected in how I dress for church. For the purposes of this discussion, my views on this are not relevant and, in my opinion, would fall under the heading of 'disputable matters' and, as such, are not worth mentioning. It is worth noting that the Bible tells us that 'If anyone, then, knows the good they ought to do and doesn't do it, it is sin for them.'[39] So if a Christian strongly believes that it is right to dress or not dress in a particular way and they go against what they believe, then for them it is a sin."

"I have rambled on a bit to demonstrate the source of that particular

---

[38] (1 Timothy 2:9–10) "⁹ I also want the women to dress modestly, with decency and propriety, adorning themselves, not with elaborate hairstyles or gold or pearls or expensive clothes, ¹⁰ but with good deeds, appropriate for women who profess to worship God."

[39] James 4:17

perception and to show you, first of all, that it can be both right and wrong at the same time, and, second of all, that in the scheme of things, it does not matter. What matters is that you do what you believe is right before God. Now, this does not mean that you can choose to do anything that you arbitrarily believe is right before God; such belief must be based on the Scriptures."

"I have often wondered about that," Jack said. "When I was small, my parents used to put on their proverbial 'Sunday best' outfits to go to church. Now, I still pass ladies on their way to church dressed in their finest, some even wearing hats. Others go to church in jeans and sneakers. It was very confusing for me, but I take your point."

At various points in our discussions, I smiled when Jack expressed his thoughts and concerns, as I remember having these same concerns myself. I now continued my response.

"I had said that I wanted to approach this Scripture issue from two points of view. We have just discussed the first, and now I will move on to the second. There is a very high incidence of people quoting Scriptures which really do not exist."

"What do you mean they do not exist?" he asked, curiously. I have noticed that over time, his attitude had changed from one of adversarial resistance to genuine desire to seek to understand.

"Let me give you a few examples," I said. "Have you ever heard the verse quoted from the Bible which says that 'money is the root of all evil'?"

"Yes," he said. "Just about everybody knows that one."

"The only problem is that it is not in the Bible. That is not what the Bible says. What the Bible says is that the *love* of money is the root of all kinds of evil,[40]" I responded. He was genuinely surprised.

"Here is another one. 'God helps those who help themselves.' Not in the Bible. In fact, you will find that this is actually contrary to much of what the Bible teaches. 'God works in mysterious ways.' True words, but not in the Bible. If you Google this (which no doubt he will and no doubt

---

[40] 1 Timothy 6:10

many readers also will), you will find several others which we assume to be from the Bible but are not."

"Including one which you used a short while ago," I said with a smile.

"Me?" he said as he sat up in his seat, "what did I say?" he asked.

"Do you remember quoting the Scripture 'God will not give you more than you can handle'?" I asked him.

He was very much taken aback by this. "But I hear it all the time," he said, "even from Christians. I used to hear my grandmother say it."

I recognized that I was drifting into "sacred" territory now. It was okay for me to challenge Charles Darwin, Richard Dawkins, and other scientists, but surely I was not going to challenge the ultimate authority? Grandma??? Horror of horrors!

I chuckled and tried to break it to him gently. "I am sorry to have to tell you this, but either you do not recall exactly what your grandmother said, or she made a common error. What the Scripture actually says is that God will not allow us to be tempted beyond what we can bear.[41]"

By allowing him to consider the possibility that it was his recollection that was flawed, I was able to help him keep the infallibility of the "ultimate authority" (Grandma,) intact. He did, however, concede that he was not aware of this small but significant difference in what is a very popular Scripture.

"The context of this particular Scripture," I continued, "is temptation and the Lord enabling us to deal with temptation. If you think about it for a minute, the incorrect but popular rendition that you repeated just does not make sense. Jesus and Paul were crucified. Stephen was stoned to death. With the exception of John, all of Jesus' other disciples were martyred. Countless numbers of Christians have been killed for their beliefs over the centuries, and it is still happening in some parts of the world today. Here in the West, we enjoy religious freedom without fear

---

[41] (1 Corinthians 10:13) "[13] No temptation[c] has overtaken you except what is common to mankind. And God is faithful; he will not let you be tempted[d] beyond what you can bear. But when you are tempted,[e] he will also provide a way out so that you can endure it."

of persecution, and we take it for granted. It is safe to say that all of these people who have been killed for their beliefs were faced with more than they could bear."

Jack smiled. "I had never given it any thought," he said, "but you are right. What you say makes perfect sense."

"In fact," I continued, "the Bible actually states quite explicitly that believers should expect to be persecuted for Christ's sake.[42]"

"So the short answer to that part of your question is that being a Christian does not guarantee an easy life. In fact, it is quite the contrary. In this regard, I am not just speaking about persecution and other dire and extreme circumstances, I am talking about everyday life."

Note to the reader: If by chance any of you happen to meet friends of mine and the subject should come up, please pay no attention to any assertion on their part that I am unlikely to offer a short answer to any question. That is entirely vicious slander on their part.

But, I digress.

Jack was now very interested in my last statement to him. "What do you mean by that?" he asked.

"Whenever someone makes a significant change in their lifestyle,

---

[42] (2 Timothy 3:12) "[12] In fact, everyone who wants to live a godly life in Christ Jesus will be persecuted."

(Luke 6:22) "Blessed are you when people hate you, when they exclude you and insult you and reject your name as evil, because of the Son of Man."

(Philippians 1:29) "For it has been granted to you on behalf of Christ not only to believe in him, but also to suffer for him."

(1 Peter 4:12–19) "[12] Dear friends, do not be surprised at the fiery ordeal that has come on you to test you, as though something strange were happening to you. [13] But rejoice in as much as you participate in the sufferings of Christ, so that you may be overjoyed when his glory is revealed. [14] If you are insulted because of the name of Christ, you are blessed, for the Spirit of glory and of God rests on you. [15] If you suffer, it should not be as a murderer or thief or any other kind of criminal, or even as a meddler. [16] However, if you suffer as a Christian, do not be ashamed, but praise God that you bear that name. [17] For it is time for judgment to begin with God's household; and if it begins with us, what will the outcome be for those who do not obey the gospel of God? [18]" And

"If it is hard for the righteous to be saved, what will become of the ungodly and the sinner?"

"[19] So then, those who suffer according to God's will should commit themselves to their faithful Creator and continue to do good."

there are always struggles against temptations to revert to the previous lifestyle. This is one of the reasons why so many people find it difficult to stick to diets. Recovering drug addicts and alcoholics struggle to stay away from drugs and alcohol and sometimes have to take drastic measures to resist the urges to fall back into old destructive habits. Having taken a decision to move away from those habits, the memories remain and have to be deliberately and vigorously managed in order for them to be able to maintain the new lifestyle."

"Similarly, when one becomes a Christian, one has taken a decision to reject a previous lifestyle and the attendant lifestyle choices and behaviors. But, the memories are still there. As in the case of recovering addicts, this process requires deliberate and sustained focus."

"Very few people experience a dramatic change whereby they are able to cast aside all of the old behaviors and desires. There are cases where this will happen, but even in those cases, they are still faced with the challenge of dealing with the urges and temptations. For most people, the conversion and behavioral change are a gradual process. In some cases, it can take years before significant change takes place. I have now been a Christian for close to twenty-five years, and I am still going through the change process."

"Sometimes, the challenges are obvious and can more easily be addressed. For example, if one was a habitual heavy eater or consumer of alcohol, these are open and obvious issues that can be addressed. They are challenging, but these represent challenges that can be addressed by lifestyle changes. This is where that scripture we spoke about earlier comes in.[43] It is difficult to face these temptations on our own, but when we put them before God, when we seek His grace, He helps us to deal with these temptations, and as long as we focus on Him and maintain that focus, we are able to resist these temptations."

"Are you saying that Christians do not face temptations Mike?" he asked.

---

[43] 1 Corinthians 10:13

"No, that is not what I am saying," I replied. "In fact, in some respects, Christians will face even more temptations. Being tempted is not a sin. Succumbing to the temptation is the sin. Let me give you a practical example. If you go to the beach and see young ladies in their swimsuits, you are not blind. You will notice them. Do not think that Christian men will not see them. Where the rubber meets the road is what happens next. Having seen them, it is incumbent upon you to keep your thoughts under control and not to allow your observation and admiration for God's handiwork to turn into lustful thoughts. If you are unable to keep your thoughts under control, it is at that point that it crosses over from temptation to sin. How do you keep these thoughts under control? That answer may vary from man to man, but the first step would be to stop looking at the young ladies."

He smiled as I related this example.

"Where it gets tricky is in dealing with internal struggles, sins such as pride, jealousy, envy, anger, and materialism. Because these are taking place inside of you and have been embedded over a lifetime, you may struggle with these for a very long time."

"If it is so difficult, then why do it? Why should someone go to the trouble of becoming a Christian if they are going to face all of these challenges?" he asked.

We had now arrived at a crucial point. I realized that I had to provide a good, convincing answer without resorting to some of the usual theologically inclined answers that are sometimes not well received by unbelievers.

"Good question," I responded. "As we have done before, let us take it out of the specific realm of Christianity and look at it in more general terms. Why does someone go on a diet? Why do alcoholics or addicts seek to get away from these destructive habits? Why do people spend hours and hours jogging or going to the gym? In all of these cases, the base answer is exactly the same. They recognize that whatever it is that they are doing now is not good and that they need to do something which will make them better people. They are seeking to be physically healthier and to have a better quality of life as a result. A longer life. All of these involve hard choices and struggles. No pain, no gain, right? These are difficult choices and difficult to commit to, but when you are serious about achieving the goal and reaping the benefits, you willingly embrace these challenges. I am told that some people even enjoy exercising and running."

He smiled at this point. Over the years, he had been encouraging me to exercise more regularly. I have embarked on exercise programs from time to time, but I find it difficult to enjoy pain for the sake of pain (that's my spin on it), and my exercise program does not last very long. I am quite happy to play football (the real football), tennis, squash, or other sports that I play with much enthusiasm not necessarily accompanied by a particularly high level of competence. These I will play to the point of exhaustion, but running miles at a time…, I am afraid that I just do not see the appeal of this.

But again…

I continued. "When you become a Christian, you have looked at your life and have recognized that there are spiritual shortcomings that you need to address. In the same way that someone commits to physical lifestyle changes to improve their health, as a Christian, you are happy to seek to achieve spiritual changes, knowing that what you are seeking to do is secure everlasting life rather than just longer life here on earth. *You also have the confidence that even though you face challenges and temptations, God will help you to deal with them.*"

I did stray into slightly deeper waters than I wanted to at this stage, but I thought it necessary to make the point. I was also confident that by now, Jack knew enough about Christianity to have an idea of what I was talking about, even though he no doubt would still have a lot of questions.

Note to the reader:

This one is a little different from my usual notes. You will recall that some chapters earlier, we discussed how God speaks to us. I thought that I would briefly share with you an experience that I had just as I was writing this section of the manuscript.

I woke up before 4:00 am, and after tossing and turning for a while, I got up and went into my home office work area and sat in front of my desk. I spent some time reading some Scriptures and praying, committing my day to the Lord, a process which we refer to as our daily devotions. After this, I checked my emails to a look at one or two emails which had come in overnight and then moved on to the writing process.

As I was finishing the section above, I thought that I should include a footnote with a Scripture which describes how we depend on God to help us face challenges. I had not yet finished the narrative, so I made a mental note to look for a verse of Scripture a little later. I then noticed that there were a few new incoming emails which I paused to check.

One of them was from one of the daily devotional services that I subscribe to, this one providing the "Bible verse of the day." The verse for that day was Titus 2:11–12, and it reads as follows:

> *[11] For the grace of God has appeared that offers salvation to all people. [12] It teaches us to say "No" to ungodliness and worldly passions, and to live self-controlled, upright and godly lives in this present age.*

I kid you not!

The creative process involves research and note-making and, of course, committing the whole process to God for his guidance.[44] The primary goal of this book is to present information which will hopefully remove barriers which are preventing non-believers from considering Christianity. It was not intended to actually convert anyone per se (although as stated earlier, it is my hope that some may take that step as a result of reading it), but rather to facilitate rational evaluation of specific facts and allow these facts to speak for themselves. With that in mind, I have attempted to minimize deep spirituality as I recognize that this might not be well received by those who are non-believers, and I did not

---

[44] (Proverbs 3:5–6) "[5] Trust in the Lord with all your heart, and lean not on your own understanding; [6] In all your ways acknowledge Him, And He shall direct your paths" (NKJV).

want to drive them away. In this regard, you will note that most of the references to Scriptures are done in footnotes, giving the reader the option to read them or not.

To some degree, this particular readers' note goes against the grain of the book. It was such a significant event in my opinion that not only did I think that I should include it, but rather, I think that God was leading me to include it. To be clear, I did not hear a Morgan Freeman (or James Earl Jones) voice telling me to include it, but when I saw how the events aligned themselves, it left no doubt in my mind that it was the Lord speaking to me and that He wanted me to pass this on to you readers.

"What is Mike making such a fuss about?" you might ask. This is clearly just a coincidence.

Well, let's look at the incidents. First, I got up out of my bed a little before 4:00 am. For me, that is prime time. Prime sleep time to be more precise. As a rule, the only time I am up at 4:00 am is if I have a flight to catch. Second, I decided to work on the book rather than browse the Internet or watch TV for a little as I sometimes do when I cannot sleep. Third, I had literally just completed the particular section dealing with the matter at hand and had a passing thought about finding a Scripture reference later in the day. Fourth, I decided to recheck my email at this point. Remember, I had checked it about an hour earlier and was not expecting anything earth-shattering, so there really was no need to recheck it. Fifth, there are thousands of Scriptures in the Bible. More than thirty-one thousand verses and this one pops up at this precise time.

It gets even better (depending on your perspective). A few paragraphs above, I mentioned that the Scripture from Titus was from one of the devotionals that I subscribe to. As I was writing this, "a little voice told me" to look at another one which came in around the same time this morning, so I stopped writing and had a look. The Scripture quoted was *Romans 6:12*. I had a look at *Romans 6:12* and the verses that follow and they read as follows:

[12]{.sup} Therefore do not let sin reign in your mortal body so that you obey its evil desires. [13] Do not offer any part of yourself to sin as an instrument of wickedness, but rather offer yourselves to God as those who have been brought from death to life; and offer every part of yourself to him as an instrument of righteousness.[14] For sin shall no longer be your master, because you are not under the law, but under grace.

Shhh! Do you hear that sound? That is the sound of my mind being blown! Could all of this be a coincidence? Let me repeat what I wrote about coincidence in an earlier chapter:

When there is an overwhelming incidence of coincidence, it argues overwhelmingly against the coincidence of the incidents.

So, coincidence? I think not. Then if not coincidence, then what? I will leave that for you to come to your own conclusion. You already know what my thoughts on it are.

Now back to poor Jack who has been in suspended animation for a few pages now, without even knowing it.

"You are saying that Christians willingly take on these struggles, knowing what is coming?" he asked.

"Here again, I must say both yes and no. There are those who understand what Christianity entails for the present and the future. These go into it with full realization of the challenges, looking forward to an eternal reward. I do not have statistics on this, but if I had to guess, I would say that these are in the minority. The vast majority, I suspect, do not fully realize what is ahead when they embrace Christianity. Many of these, as they become mature Christians, eventually realize what is ahead and willingly face the challenges, with the Lord at their side. There are those, though, who do not quite make the adjustment and they struggle."

"If you look at many of the non-Judeo-Christian religions around the world, you will see that what they have in common is that they worship their god(s) for what the god(s) can do for them. That seems to be the primary focus. Hence religions which have a multiplicity of gods have gods for every kind of need that you can think of. Rain gods, fertility gods, agriculture gods, and the list is endless. Some people approach Christianity in the same way, but Christianity is different. Yes, our God will bless us, but that is not His primary objective. His primary objective is the establishment of His Everlasting Kingdom at some point in the future, and our goal should be to do what we need to do to participate in that eternal Kingdom. There are Scriptures which affirm that God will bless us, but in those Scriptures, the stated or implied underlying condition is that we must be acting in accordance with His will.[45]"

Jack nodded his head as he contemplated this. He seemed to be deep in thought, and I did not disturb him. After a few minutes, he said to me: "Mike, I want you to listen carefully to what I am about to say so that you do not misunderstand me."

I smiled and waited for him to continue.

"When we had our first conversation, I was actually doing it for the sake of debating. I had unyielding views on religion and was resolute in my convictions." He paused before continuing as he tried to carefully put together what he wanted to say.

"Little by little, my approach to the discussions changed, and it has reached a point now where many of my views have changed. I would like to thank you for helping me work through this process slowly and rationally, and I think that I am now ready to personally dig a little deeper. Just to be clear, I am not saying that I want to become a Christian at this point but that I no longer find the idea to be abhorrent."

I listened in silence as he continued.

"I am not convinced of the Adam and Eve story or that the earth was created in seven days. I am not even sure that I am convinced of the existence of God. Having said that though, the points that you made about

---

[45] (Hebrews 10:35–36) "[35] So do not throw away your confidence; it will be richly rewarded. [36] You need to persevere so that when you have done the will of God, you will receive what he has promised."

the 'still small voice' I found to be very compelling. I was also very interested in what you said about Christianity as compared to other religions and the expectations of the adherents of these religions. That has given me a clearer perspective on a number of things."

"What I would like to do now is to take my inquiries one step further. I have been to church on occasion and even accompanied my wife to a Bible study some time ago. In retrospect, my approach to both church and Bible study was one of ridicule and criticism, but now my perception of both is quite different. What advice can you give me as to how to go forward from here?"

I resisted the urge to smile and said to him, "Jack, I would like to commend you on your approach to these discussions. You promised that you would give me a fair hearing and not to hold the discussions to an artificially high standard. You have delivered on your promises. We covered a lot of ground, and I am happy that you are interested in investigating further."

"First of all, I suggest you get a good study Bible. A study Bible is a Bible which has explanatory notes and articles to help you to understand the Scriptures. I can recommend one to you when you are ready to purchase it."

He nodded as I continued.

"Next, it would be useful if you could get into some formal Bible study. You could go with your wife if you wish. Alternatively, I meet with a group of young Christian men every Monday. You are welcome to join us. The environment is very nonthreatening, and our discussions are very interesting."

"I would like that," he said.

And so dear reader, the objective has been accomplished. The barriers have been broken down. Jack has not embraced Christianity. Yet. But he has taken a great leap forward. Will he embrace it in the future? At this stage, we do not know. Perhaps after a series of Bible studies, he might. Perhaps we will find out in a subsequent volume…

But I digress.

Epilogue

My first venture at university was interrupted when I decided to enter and stay in the working world. Some may say that I dropped out of university, but I think that would be a rather harsh description of the events. What happened is that I switched my academic pursuits from a BSc in Physics and/or Chemistry to a professional qualification in my "chosen" field, insurance, property and casualty (or general) insurance to be more specific. The astute reader will no doubt have noticed that the word "chosen" above is enclosed in quotation marks. This is a nod to the fact that in almost forty years of insurance experience, I have only met three people who admit to choosing a career in insurance. In all three cases, an insurance executive parent was lurking in the background who no doubt intentionally or unintentionally influenced their decisions. As such, to say that this was my "chosen" profession is stretching it a bit. I fell into insurance by accident just like everybody else (except for those three).

Fast-forward eight or nine years. At this point, I had been married for about six years, had two children, and held a management position at a leading insurance company. I decided that having studied insurance for several years, it was time for me to supplement my on-the-job experience with some formal management training, and as such, I enrolled in a part-time Management Studies program through the University of the West Indies.

One of the courses that we had to do was Sociology, an unknown quantity to me at the time, but I eventually got the hang of it. At some point in this course, we were assigned the task of writing about Max Weber. This was in the days before computers became popular and readily accessible, and as such, the writing of papers was done in the old-fashioned way, using a pen. This, of course, makes the process of editing more difficult, and invariably, the quality of the end product suffered.

I received a "B" for my efforts and was very surprised when my lecturer informed me that they wished to publish my essay in the department's scholarly journal! Yes, I am a published scholar! No, I do not have a copy of the journal, so you will have to take my word for it (it was thirty years ago. Give me a break!). He said it was highly unusual for them to publish a paper which only earned a "B" but that it was such a strong paper that they felt compelled to make an exception. He said it was a very strong paper right up to near the end at which point it seemed as if I ran out of time (or steam) and just decided to bring it to an abrupt end. That was why I got a "B" instead of an "A."

And that was *EXACTLY* what happened.

I was working on it, and eventually, the challenge of writing this long paper by hand took a toll on me (remember I was working full time and had a young family). So I brought it to a premature close. And earned my "B." My published "B."

Do you see where I am going with this?

So, dear readers, with this story now on the table, some of you may think that the same thing happened with this book. You may think that I just got tired of writing about my conversations with Jack and decided to bring it to a close. Well, that is not so.

If you go back to the early part of the book, you will see that my intention with this book was not to lead Jack (or you for that matter) to a decision to embrace Christianity and that I made no overt attempt to do so. The objective was to break down barriers which were preventing Jack (or you for that matter) from being able to consider Christianity rationally. If you look at how the conversations came to an end, you will note that that is exactly where Jack is now. He has, over a period of several weeks, reviewed his long-held positions and has recognized that some of them needed to be changed. I sincerely hope that some of you will also find yourselves in a similar situation, one where you recognize that some of your preconceived notions are worthy or re-evaluation.

Please note that I have not asked you to change these notions or to admit that they are wrong. All that I ask is that you re-evaluate them in an as unbiased way as it is possible to evaluate subject matter which is inherently subject to bias, one way or the other. If you are willing to do that, to honestly do that, then regardless of the outcome of your re-evaluation, the objective of this book will have been achieved.

As it currently stands, my plan is to follow Jack's progress as he continues along his quest. This may be the subject of future books in this series.

Of course, it is my hope and prayer that some of you will have been further along than Jack was and are now ready to embrace Christianity as a result of this book.

It is not my place to convert anyone. My job is to plant the seed and let God do the rest.

Blessings,
Michael C. Gayle
Conversations With My Unbelieving Friend

CPSIA information can be obtained
at www.ICGtesting.com
Printed in the USA
LVHW080002050820
662053LV00010B/4